To Clarence

In partial payment
for the love of my life.

Lee
12/25/77

**Benefit-Cost Analysis:
A Practical Guide**

Benefit-Cost Analysis: A Practical Guide

Lee G. Anderson
Russell F. Settle
University of Delaware

Lexington Books
D.C. Heath and Company
Lexington, Massachusetts
Toronto

Library of Congress Cataloging in Publication Data

Anderson, Lee G
  Benefit-cost analysis.

  Bibliography: p.
  Includes index.
  1. Cost effectiveness. I. Settle, Russell F., joint author. II. Title.
HD47.A268   658.1'552   77-3108
ISBN 0-669-01465-6

Published simultaneously in Canada.

Printed in the United States of America.

International Standard Book Number: 0-669-01465-6

Library of Congress Catalog Card Number: 77-3108

To the University of
Delaware economics faculty
seminar on game theory,
risk analysis, and
income redistribution.

Contents

List of Figures

List of Tables

Acknowledgments

We would like to thank Joel Goodman for encouraging us to undertake this project, Josephine Palmer for her cheerful attitude throughout the typing of several drafts of the manuscript, and students at the University of Delaware who used this material in a preliminary form and provided useful suggestions.

Benefit-Cost Analysis:
A Practical Guide

1 Introduction

Overview

Federal, state, and local governments spend hundreds of billions of dollars annually on a wide variety of public sector activities. In addition, governments at all levels regulate the behavior of individuals and businesses: there are literally hundreds of government agencies engaged in the regulation of private commerce. Governments organize, control, or influence the use of enormous quantities of productive resources. The problem is, how can policymakers determine whether their decisions affecting the use of these productive resources are, in fact, in the public interest? Benefit-cost analysis is one important decision-making aid that will often generate the information necessary to determine whether a given public sector activity is desirable or whether it constitutes a waste of society's productive resources.

In general terms, benefit-cost analysis is a tool for systematically developing useful information about the desirable and undesirable effects of public sector programs or projects. In a sense, benefit-cost analysis is the public sector analog to the private sector's profitability analysis: the former attempts to determine whether social benefits of a proposed public sector activity outweigh the social costs whereas the latter attempts to determine whether the private benefits (that is, revenue) of a proposed private sector investment outweigh the private costs. Examples of benefit-cost analyses include studies on air pollution control, consumer protection legislation, education programs, prison reform, the trans-Alaska pipeline, airport noise, disease control, infant nutrition, recreation facilities, labor and manpower training programs, housing programs, and many more.

A fairly extensive list of readings on both the theoretical and practical level can be found at the end of this book. It is not meant to be a complete reference to benefit-cost–related material, but it does provide a good representation of the types of studies that are available and in what types of publications they can be found. Obviously, a list such as this becomes outdated quite fast and the reader who is interested in keeping up with current studies will find the *Journal of Economic Literature,* under the classification of welfare theory and social choice (024 and 025 respectively), a very useful source.

Benefit-cost analysis can be divided into four main stages: identification, classification, quantification, and presentation. The identification stage involves identifying and listing all the various effects of a proposed project or program. In

1

principle, this set of effects provides the benefit-cost analyst with a checklist of all the items that should be taken into consideration. The second main stage entails classifying these various effects into economic-efficiency benefits and costs (for example, desirable project outputs and productive resources used in a project) and income-distributional effects. There will be some overlap between efficiency and distributional effects. The third stage involves quantification wherever feasible of both the economic-efficiency benefits and costs and the income-distributional impacts of the project. The final major stage of a benefit-cost analysis is presentation of the relevant information in a reasonably straight-forward manner—in a form that clearly spells out the important assumptions underlying the analysis and the implications of those assumptions for the study's conclusions. The information presentation part of a benefit-cost analysis is often a weak link in the chain, and interpretation of the results is therefore sometimes quite difficult. In addition, it often means that the work of different individuals on the same project may not be easily compared. Consequently, we will place special emphasis on the information presentation stage.

This book has two purposes. First, it attempts to provide a basic under-standing of the theoretic foundations of benefit-cost analysis. Second, and perhaps more importantly, it seeks to demonstrate the application of benefit-cost analysis in realistic (and less-than-ideal) situations, for example, those involving incomplete data or time and budget constraints. The need for a book like this arises because the usual textbook presentation of benefit-cost analysis fails to adequately bridge the gap between the underlying economic theory and the correct application of benefit-cost principles in an actual study.

Benefit-cost analysis derives directly from theoretic welfare economics, a subject normally reserved for fairly advanced treatments of economic theory. To avoid errors in the classification and measurement of benefits and costs, it is clearly necessary to understand and, thus, for this book to discuss the the-oretic aspects of benefit-cost analysis. However, it is not necessary to present these underlying principles within the context of advanced economic theory. The present book discusses the theoretic aspects in as simple and straightforward a manner as possible. Our objective is to provide a treatment of benefit-cost analysis understandable not only to the economics student, but also the practi-tioner who may have little or no formal training in economics.

Although the analogy is less than perfect, writing a book on benefit-cost analysis is somewhat like writing simple instructions for setting a broken arm for non-M.D.s. The actual process of setting the bone so that it will heal properly may be quite simple. However, the general knowledge required of the body and how it works, especially when there are complications, is quite enormous. This is probably why most doctors would be hesitant to provide laymen with more than first-aid information, that is, what to do until the doctor comes. Any specific advice would contain cautions about letting a professional do the work if at all possible and would also include a listing of any danger signs that would necessitate professional help in order to do a satisfactory job.

It is true that the practice of medicine and of performing benefit-cost analysis are really quite different things, but nevertheless it is useful to compare the two. For one thing, the latter is not so difficult that there is anything in it directly analogous to first aid. Indeed it is one of the tenets of this book that useful analysis is possible in many cases with only a basic understanding of welfare economics and of some other economic tools and concepts. On the other hand in more complicated cases or in instances where there is a lack of critical economic data (elasticities of demand and so on), it will be necessary to use a professional with full knowledge of economic and econometric analysis at his disposal in order to obtain meaningful results. Since it would be impossible to include enough information in this short book to transform the reader into such a professional, our goal will be to provide the basics, to show how to use them, and to provide a series of danger signs that indicate that more advanced assistance will be necessary.

The outline of this book is as follows. The first chapter discusses the relationship of benefit-cost analysis to modern welfare economics. Chapter 2 focuses on social benefits and costs. It begins with a discussion of the underlying economic theory and proceeds to a consideration of how and when these theoretic concepts should actually be applied. Chapter 3 addresses the issue of comparing present benefits and costs with those occurring in the future. The present-value concept is introduced and the notions of market and social discount rates are considered.

Chapter 4 extends the analysis to include risk and uncertainty and considers approaches to incorporating distributional impacts and intangible effects into benefit-cost analyses. Chapter 5 brings all of the preceding material together: it demonstrates the proper ways to manipulate, organize, and display the information about benefits and costs and their distribution so as to provide the most useful information to policymakers.

An Illustration

Before turning to a more formal discussion of benefit-cost analysis, it will prove useful to present an overview of the subject by means of a simple example that focuses on the economic efficiency implications of a hypothetical water development project. For simplicity, income distribution aspects will be ignored in this example. In particular, we are interested in determining which project effects are efficiency (or social) benefits and which are efficiency (or social) costs. The efficiency benefit of a project is the value of the goods and services provided by that project, whereas the efficiency cost (often referred to as *opportunity cost*) of a project is the value of the goods and services foregone as a result of the project. In both instances, "value" is measured (in principle) by individuals' true *willingness to pay* for the goods and services involved. (These concepts are discussed in more detail below; these brief definitions are set forth here to facilitate discussion of the example.)

The Problem. Consider a proposed multipurpose dam that will provide electricity, a lake suitable for recreation, and a bridge. The following information details all of the relevant effects of the dam.

1. The total cost of constructing the dam is $5,000,000 (for land, labor, and capital) of which $500,000, $1,000,000, and $2,000,000 are directly attributable to the bridge, the recreation facility, and the hydroelectric plant, respectively. The remaining $1,500,000 expenditure, while necessary, is not directly attributable to any of the three projects individually. Of this non-attributable amount, $500,000 is for unskilled labor, 20 percent of whom will be drawn from an unemployed pool of labor in the area.

2. Currently, transportation across the river is handled by a ferry company which provides 1,000,000 passenger crossings a year. The average cost (to the firm) per passenger crossing is thirty cents; the fee charged each passenger is forty cents. Since economists include a normal profit as part of production costs, the ten-cent difference between revenue and costs is an *economic profit*. If the fee were to fall to thirty cents, the ferry company would still find it profitable to operate; the economic profit involves payments over and above that which would be necessary to get the ferry service provided. The authority that will operate the bridge has stated that there will be a toll of twenty cents per vehicle. It has been estimated that at this lower price per crossing the annual number of crossings will increase from 1,000,000 to 1,200,000. Annual bridge operating costs are assumed to be zero.

3. The recreation facility, which will have an annual maintenance cost of $50,000, is expected to attract 500,000 visitors per year who will spend $40,000 annually on equipment and supplies to use at the recreation site. Although there are no plans to charge an admission fee, it was determined that the number of visitors per year would fall in the following way if admission fees were used.

Fee	Annual visitors per year
$ 0	500,000
.50	400,000
1.00	300,000
1.50	200,000
2.00	100,000
2.50	0

This table is a demand schedule for the recreation facility. It shows how many visitors will use the park each year at different fees, other things equal. Alternatively this schedule can be interpreted as showing that of the 500,000 that would show up with no fee, 400,000 would have been willing to pay fifty cents rather than do without this recreational opportunity. Similarly 300,000 of them would have been willing to pay $1.00; 200,000 of them would have been willing to pay $1.50 and so on.

4. The electric generating facility, which will cost $1,000,000 annually to operate, is expected to produce 3,000,000 kilowatts per year, which is less than one percent of current production of power in the area. Consumers currently pay forty cents per kilowatt hour.

5. An individual who rents canoes at a nearby lake has announced plans to move his operations to the new facility if it is built. During the previous year this firm had revenues of $7,000 but had to pay wages of $3,000 and purchase supplies worth $2,000, which left $2,000 for the owner's salary and for wear and tear on the rental boats. The owner expects that business will be about the same in the new location.

Using the above information it is possible to answer the following questions. What are the costs? What are the net annual benefits? (Remember that we have put a special meaning on the terms *benefits* and *costs* and it is this interpretation that must be used.) Should the project as a whole be undertaken, or only certain parts? The answers provided below will be quite brief because each concept is discussed in detail in the sections to follow. Also, remember that for purposes of this discussion, it is assumed that the above list includes all of the relevant effects of the dam.

What are the Costs? If the market economy is doing its job properly, the social cost of constructing the facility will simply be equal to the budgetary outlay for the land, labor, and capital inputs employed. In order to obtain the productive inputs they have to be bid away from other uses. Provided that productive factors are paid approximately the value of their marginal product, then the payments necessary to bid productive inputs away from other pursuits provide a measure of the value of the goods and services that could have been produced in those other pursuits. (We will describe below how a properly operating market economy can provide information on both social benefits and social costs and how information provided by the market should be corrected when there are imperfections.) The use of unemployed workers requires us to qualify this point somewhat. Since those workers would not have been employed without the project, the social opportunity cost (the value of foregone production) from using them in this project is zero. Society does not give up any goods or services by using them in the construction of the dam because they would have otherwise been unemployed. Thus, the financial cost of the project has to be modified in order to come up with an estimate of the opportunity cost of the project.

Since 20 percent of the unskilled workers were unemployed and the total wage bill for these workers is $500,000, only 80 percent of this expenditure measures foregone production, or, to put it another way, 20 percent, or $100,000, does not really represent a social opportunity cost. Therefore, financial costs must be reduced from $5,000,000 to $4,900,000 in order to obtain the correct measure of total social costs. Therefore, although $5,000,000 is the dollar cost of the dam, the social opportunity cost is only $4,900,000 because that is the estimated value of other goods and services that could have been produced by the productive inputs had the dam not been built.

What are the Net Annual Benefits? There are three types of services produced by the dam, and so there will be three types of benefits. Recall that the benefits of a project are defined as the value of the goods or services produced. Each of the outputs of the project will be discussed in turn.

Bridge. The correct measure of benefits from the bridge can best be calculated by looking separately at the current number of crossings and the expected increase in crossings. With respect to the former, the average cost of providing the original 1,000,000 passenger crossings by the ferry is thirty cents. This means that with the construction of the bridge, $300,000 worth of productive inputs that were previously used by the ferry company can be transferred to other uses where they can produce goods and services worth $300,000. This is a measure of the benefits provided because of the current transportation load being picked up by the bridge. An alternative way to look at this point is to note that the services provided the original users were worth at least $400,000 ($.40 times 1,000,000 crossings). However, since the ferry operator is put out of business by the bridge, he loses the $100,000 a year he used to earn in pure economic profits. Therefore, part of the gain to current consumers is a transfer from the ferry operator. Thus, the net gain is $300,000 which is the value of the resources released because the ferry company is no longer in business.

The bridge reduces the price for crossing the river and, consequently, generates 200,000 extra trips per year. How should these additional crossings be valued? Since the users are willing to pay (at a minimum) a toll of twenty cents per crossing for the extra crossings, their value must be at least equal to $40,000 ($.20 times the 200,000 extra trips). But the total value is likely to be higher than this amount because without the bridge the last trip had a value of forty cents (because that is what the marginal user was willing to pay the ferry operator to cross). The first new trip would therefore provide twenty cents in extra value. They were willing to pay forty cents but the toll is only twenty cents. The last additional crossing provides no extra value because the willingness to pay is equal to the toll. If we take an average of these two values and multiply it times the number of new trips, we will have an estimate of the value to consumers of the 200,000 additional crossings over and above what they actually paid. This value, called consumers' surplus, is $20,000 ($.10 times 200,000 crossings). The total annual benefits to new users is $60,000, $40,000 of which they actually pay and $20,000 of which they receive as a surplus.

The aggregate annual benefits are the sum of the benefits to the current users and those to the new users, or $360,000. Since (by assumption) there are no operating costs for the bridge, this amount also measures the net annual benefits.

It is interesting to point out that there is a difference between the private return to the project and its social benefit. The revenues from the toll are $240,000. This is how much people have to pay for the services of the bridge but it does not represent the value produced. This is a good point to keep in mind—a social benefit-cost analysis does not provide a measure of the business profitability of a project; it is concerned with the social benefits and costs associated with a project. Whether benefits, for example, are in fact captured as a revenue to the agency involved is of no importance as far as economic efficiency is concerned, although it may be important as far as income distribution or practical financing problems are concerned.

Recreation Facility. The benefits from the recreation facility depend upon the value of the services provided by the facility. Therefore, in order to measure the benefits we require some notion of people's willingness to pay for those recreational services. The fact that $40,000 is spent annually on equipment and supplies in order to utilize the lake is not an appropriate measure of this willingness to pay and, thus, should be ignored. The production of these items require the use of resources that could have produced $40,000 worth of goods and services elsewhere in the economy; therefore, to classify this expenditure as a benefit of the lake would be to ignore the resource cost of producing the equipment and supplies. In a similar vein, the activity of the boat rental firm cannot be considered a social benefit of the project, even though it may have an impact on the users of the recreational facility. This effect is not a social benefit because the beneficial services being provided at the new facility are just offset by the reduction in those same services at the other lake. Therefore, as far as the whole economy is concerned, this effect does not entail a net gain in the value of goods and services produced. Only the location of production has changed. This type of effect is called a *secondary* or *parochial benefit,* and as a general rule should not be counted in efficiency calculations.

What is needed is an estimate of the value of recreational activity over and above what it costs (in terms of resources) to participate in it. This can be obtained using the information in paragraph 3 above. The problem is analogous to that of measuring the extra value of the newly generated trips across the river. Notice that with no admission fee, there would be 500,000 visitors. If the price were raised to fifty cents the number of visitors would fall to 400,000. This means that there is at least a willingness to pay of $200,000 for the facility, because of the 500,000 original visitors, 400,000 will remain at a fifty-cent fee. Note, however, that if the price is raised to $1.00 the number of visitors falls to 300,000. This means that these 300,000 individuals would be willing to pay fifty cents more than was counted in the original $200,000. Therefore, we must add another $150,000 to the total. Along the same line when the price goes up to $1.50, 200,000 individuals are still willing to participate even with the fifty-cent increase in price. This means that another $100,000 must be added to the total. Finally, since 100,000 would still remain if the price were raised another fifty cents, we must add a final $50,000 to our estimate of total willingness to pay for the facility. If the price goes up another fifty cents, attendance falls to zero. If we add all of these amounts we obtain $500,000 as an estimate of the value of the recreational services provided by the lake. This estimate implies that if all of the visitors were forced to pay the maximum that they would be willing to pay rather than do without, a maximum of $500,000 could be collected.

Notice that if the relationship between visits and willingness to pay is assumed to be continuous, an estimate can be obtained that takes into account price changes of less than fifty cent increments. With 500,000 visitors, the willingness to pay for the last visit is zero; but as the number of visits approaches zero, willingness to pay increases to $2.50. As in the above case involving the ferry company, if we take the average of these values and multiply it by the 500,000 visitors we can obtain an estimate of the total willingness to pay for the recreational opportunities. This approach yields $625,000 ($1.25 times 500,000) as the value of the recreational services provided by the lake. For purposes of this discussion we will use this more precise amount. Note again, however, regardless of the estimate employed, there is a difference between the project's revenues and its social benefits. In this case the recreational facility generates no revenues but provides $625,000 worth of gross social benefits per year. Taking into account the $50,000 maintenance costs, the net annual benefits are $575,000.

Electricity. Since the output of electricity is so small relative to current electricity production in the region, there will likely be no change in the price of electricity. Therefore, there is little difficulty determining the social benefit of this part of the project. The current market price is forty cents per kilowatt and the output will be 3,000,000 kilowatts per year. The social value of the output will therefore be $1,200,000 per year. Taking into account the $1,000,000 annual operating costs leaves net social benefit of $200,000 a year.

Overall Evaluation. Should the project be approved? In order to answer this question we must determine whether the stream of net annual benefits from all three uses through time is high enough to merit the opportunity cost of $4,900,000 in lost production necessary to undertake the project. Because people prefer a given amount of benefits in the present over an equal amount of benefits sometime in the future (How else can we explain the existence of interest payments to entice people to lend?) it is necessary to translate all future values into present values to determine whether the benefits of this project exceed the costs. The standard method for performing this translation is to discount values in the future back to a present value equivalent. (Discounting is discussed in considerable detail in chapter 3, but in order to keep this illustration simple, we will make some temporarily undefended assertions about discounting.) In essence, the present-value equivalent of some future value to be received n years from now is the amount of money one would have to invest today in order to generate that future value by the nth year. For example, consider the present value of $100 to be received in exactly one year. If one could invest money today at a 5 percent compound rate of interest, one could generate $100 by the end of a year by investing $95.24 today; that is, the present value of $100 one year from now is $95.24 provided the discount rate is 5 percent. If one could earn a 10 percent rate of interest on money invested today, then the present value of the $100 one year from now would be $90.91. Thus, we see that the present value of any future sum is inversely related to the discount rate (that is, the rate of return that could be earned if one invested funds today).

Let us suppose that 10 percent is the appropriate discount rate for this hypothetical project. Given this information and the estimates of the net annual benefits, we could show—but for simplicity we will simply assert for now—that the present values of the annual net benefit streams over, say, the first fifteen years are $2,737,800 for the bridge, $4,372,875 for the recreation facility, and $1,521,000 for the hydroelectric plant. (We could obviously carry the calculations further than fifteen years, but this time period is adequate for the purposes of this example.)

The sum of the present values of the three services is $8,631,675. Therefore, considering the project as a unit, it makes sense on efficiency grounds to approve it because the present value of the net benefits for the first fifteen years is more than enough to cover the $4,900,000 opportunity cost of building it. The difference between the total discounted benefits and costs, otherwise known as the *net present value,* is $3,731,675. In other words, a net social gain can be obtained by reallocating resources from other uses into the construction of this project because the value of the goods and services obtained by doing so is greater than the value of the goods and services foregone.

Since this is a multipurpose project each of the individual parts should also be examined. The present value of the benefits and that part of the cost that is directly attributable to each are presented below.

	Present Value of Benefits	*Attributable Cost*
Bridge	2,737,800	500,000
Recreation	4,372,875	1,000,000
Electricity	1,521,000	2,000,000

Both the bridge and the recreational facility generate more than enough benefits to cover their attributable costs but this is not so for the hydroelectric plant. This result implies that, even though the whole project as a unit appears efficient, one component of the overall project would represent an inefficient use of resources. The net present value of the project would increase from $3,731,675 to $4,210,675 if the hydroelectric plant is not built. Admittedly, $1,521,000 worth of discounted benefits would be lost, but social costs would also fall by $2,000,000 yielding a net savings of $479,000.

Concluding Remarks. This example demonstrates that there is more to a benefit-cost analysis than many people assume. In fact, many readers may be quite surprised at some of the things that were included as well as those which were left out. In fact, if your first inclination is to disagree with the reasoning presented above, you probably are not in the minority. We hope, however, that as the discussion proceeds the reasoning will become more clear. The example was simple as far as dollar amounts are concerned but it was complex as far as the number of important economic issues are concerned. It is likely, however, that the example is fairly representative of many of the types of projects that governments must consider and of the difficult issues that must be faced. For example, one must always beware of unemployed resources and of transfers that appear to be benefits. Also there are many ways of placing values on the relevant outputs. In some instances it is proper to use alternative cost (as in the case of the bridge), in others the existing market price may be used (the electric facility), and in still others estimates of the demand curve must be obtained (the recreation project). The example of a project related to water usage is quite appropriate because a good deal of early benefit-cost analysis was in this field. However, it is a tool that can be used to study the efficiency and income distribution effects of almost any type of project or program.

The Basis for Benefit-Cost Analysis

Economic Efficiency

Although the phrase *benefit-cost analysis* can have a variety of meanings to noneconomists it has a special, well-defined meaning to economists in general and benefit-cost analysts in particular. In this section we discuss the underlying economic principles upon which the economists' notion of benefit-cost analysis rests.

Economics is the study of the allocation of scarce resources among competing uses. Welfare economics is that branch of economics that focuses on the question of how a society can allocate those scarce resources so as to maximize social welfare. Or, put differently, welfare economics is concerned with the formulation of criteria that will allow decisionmakers to distinguish between those activities, programs, or projects that would make society better off and those that would make it worse off. Benefit-cost analysis is *applied* welfare economics; that is, it entails the application of the principles of welfare economics to specific and actual activities, programs, or projects.

The fundamental issue of welfare economics is how to determine whether a society has been made better off or worse off. Economists resolve this issue into two components, economic efficiency and income-distributional equity. At this point, we restrict our attention for the most part to the economic efficiency component.

With respect to the economic efficiency criterion, an activity enhances a society's welfare if that activity results in a net increase in the value of the goods and services produced throughout the economy. Conversely, a society's well-being is diminished, from an economic efficiency point of view, if an activity reduces the value of the goods and services produced. The value of the goods and services produced by the economy is measured by the yardstick of people's actual *willingness to pay* for those goods and services (economic demand). The efficiency benefits and costs of public sector activities ultimately depend upon individuals' willingness to pay. To illustrate, for a project to generate, say, $1 million of efficiency benefits, it must necessarily be the case that individuals, in the aggregate, are willing to pay up to a maximum of $1 million for the project's output rather than do without. Alternatively, for a project to entail, say, $2 million in efficiency costs, it must necessarily be the case that individuals, in the aggregate, are willing to pay up to (but not more than) $2 million rather than give up the goods and services that would be foregone were the project to be undertaken.

Although willingness to pay is a very useful measure of value, it does have some important characteristics that should be explicitly noted. First, it assumes that people know what is good for them. Some might argue with this assumption, citing drug addiction or perhaps the relative expenditures on alcoholic beverages compared with expenditures on education as proof that there is reason to believe differently. The only rebuttal is that if individuals do not know what is good for them, who does? Can we find a benevolent dictator who could make all of the allocation decisions such that only those goods that were "good" for us could be obtained and that they would be produced in the "right" proportions?

Another problem is that willingness to pay is directly related to the distribution of income. Using the criteria of economic efficiency, a desire is counted for nothing unless it is backed with money to translate it into an actual willingness to pay. If the distribution of income were changed, it is highly likely that the relative weights (in a willingness-to-pay sense) given to the different goods would change also; different people would now have the income to back up their tastes.

The fact that the willingness-to-pay criterion is so closely tied to the distribution of income is very important. However, because economists have no way of determining which distribution is superior or exactly how willingness to pay would change if another distribution were adopted, they resort to using the existing income distribution as the standard.

To summarize the above two points, for basic economic analysis most economists have accepted the value judgments that individuals are the best judges of their satisfaction and that the existing distribution of income can be accepted as a basis for economic analysis. These underlying assumptions should be kept in mind, however, whenever policy recommendations are made.

A final problem with the willingness-to-pay criterion is that there are no markets for some goods and services. For example, individuals may have a high willingness to pay for clean air, but there is no practical way for this demand to be translated into actual purchases of clean air in the private marketplace. Thus, it will be difficult—though certainly not impossible—to obtain measures of the economic value that people place on clean air. Similarly, there may be a relatively high willingness to pay for the services rendered by an undeveloped stretch of shore property. For instance, individuals may obtain considerable satisfaction from the natural scenery and they may be willing to give up some money in order to keep the land undeveloped. Unfortunately, it is very difficult to set up a market where such exchanges can take place. For our discussion here, this is important because the actual willingness to pay is never demonstrated; consequently, we are not able to easily measure the value that people place on such goods or services. It also means that in the case of the shore property, for example, the land may be put into a second-best use as far as society is concerned. The owner may use the land to provide goods or services that are commonly bought and sold in the market (apartment buildings, for example). If the value provided by an apartment complex is less than that of the open shore property, a suboptimal allocation of resources has occurred. The possibility of such occurrences is one of the reasons why benefit-cost analysis has developed—to provide a wider view of allocative efficiency effects than may be adopted by individuals seeking to satisfy their own private interests.

These problems of measurement notwithstanding, it is important to realize that the concept of willingness to pay does include all effects, regardless of whether they are directly market related. Therefore, as a criterion of value it is not as narrow or materialistic as it may initially seem. We are using dollars as a common denominator, but this usage does not mean that we are excluding those things that are not produced on the market. As defined above, welfare economics is the study of the allocation of scarce resources to maximize welfare, and in order to insure that welfare is actually maximized, it is essential (at least in principle) that all effects upon society's well-being be considered.

Benefit-Cost Analysis and Economic Efficiency

As noted in the preceding section, an efficient allocation of resources occurs when the total value of goods and services produced is maximized, that is, at that point where there is no way that the given set of resources (land, labor, and capital) can be reallocated such that the value of the newly produced goods or services is greater than the value of the goods or services that must be given up. Essentially, benefit-cost analysis is a tool for determining whether a specific reallocation of resources actually does increase the value of goods and services produced and hence (from an efficiency point of view) the general welfare of society.

There is one welfare economics criterion (the Pareto criterion) that suggests that an efficient allocation of resources occurs only when there are no possible reallocations that could make at least one person better off without making another worse off. It is argued that reliance upon this criterion would allow us to determine when there have been unambiguous gains (or losses) in social well-being without having to engage in interpersonal welfare comparisons (that is, having to determine whether my gain enhances my well-being more than your loss decreases your well-being). Unfortunately, this is a very restrictive criterion—there are few, if any, public sector activities that could satisfy it. Thus, reliance upon this criterion of Pareto optimality would result in very few public sector programs being undertaken on strict economic efficiency grounds.

A less restrictive criterion (called the Hicks-Kaldor criterion or potential Pareto optimality) states that an increase in general welfare occurs if those that are made better off from some change could, in principle, fully compensate those that are made worse off and still achieve an improvement in welfare. It is this criterion of economic efficiency upon which benefit-cost analysis is based. That is, if a reallocation of resources leads to a net increase in the value of goods and services produced, it is obvious that if some people are made worse off (that is, the value of the goods and services those people obtain is reduced), the fact that there is a net increase in the value of production would allow those that are made better off to compensate the losers.

This is such an important point that it bears repeating in a somewhat different way. Benefit-cost analysis is a tool for determining whether projects or programs are economically efficient, that is, whether they generate social benefits in excess of social costs without regard (at this stage) to the distribution of those benefits and costs. Projects that result in a net increase in the value of goods and services produced will receive favorable ratings by properly conceived and executed benefit-cost analyses. A favorable rating, however, does not guarantee that everyone in society will be made better off as a result. Indeed, there may be many who are made worse off by any given project. The reason the project is acceptable on economic efficiency grounds is that it would be possible, in principle, to fully compensate those who lose by transferring a part of the gain from those who have been made better off to those who have been made worse off by the project.

It is important to realize that this potential for transfers to insure that every individual in society is at least no worse off does not guarantee that such transfers will take place. Therefore, a project that would be approved on economic efficiency grounds may result in an absolute decrease in the welfare of certain individuals or groups in society. It is obvious that in addition to the efficiency aspects of public sector projects, policymakers will often be concerned with the income-distributional implications as well. We will discuss these problems in greater detail in several contexts below.

With this basic introduction, it is now possible to discuss in more detail the main elements of a benefit-cost analysis. From the viewpoint of the benefit-cost analyst, the basic criterion to be satisfied is that the value of goods and services produced be increased. Therefore, it is necessary for the analyst to determine what, and how many, goods and services will be produced as a direct result of the project under consideration and then to place the appropriate dollar value on them. These outputs are the benefits of the project. In order to produce these benefits, it is necessary to transfer resources from other productive uses in the economy. It is, therefore, necessary for the analyst to specify what kinds and amounts of goods and services will be foregone as a result of the project and then place the appropriate values on them. If after completing these measurements it is found that the value of goods and services produced (the benefits) is greater than the value of goods and services foregone (the costs) the project can be considered beneficial on efficiency grounds. To be precise, such a finding means that if the project is undertaken the net value of goods and services produced in the economy will increase and although there may be certain individuals who are made worse off, there is a potential to make everyone better off if the gains from the project are properly redistributed.

Although we have been discussing benefit-cost analysis in terms of studying a project, it is also very useful in determining the actual size of a project, such as whether a pollution control project should remove 60 percent or 70 percent of the existing pollutants. This, of course, depends upon the cost of increasing the cleansing capacity of the project and the extra benefit that will be derived. If the extra benefits are greater than the extra costs, then the 70 percent project is superior. The use of benefit-cost analysis to determine the proper size of a project is just as important as determining whether a project should be built or not. This means that proper analysis is important from the conception of a project. If economists are called in only at the end to assess the economic efficiency of a given-sized project, potential gains may be overlooked.

Note that in many ways benefit-cost analysis is analogous to profitability analysis employed in the private sector. The crucial difference between the two lies in the way gains and losses are defined. A firm is primarily concerned with those aspects of its operation that actually affect revenue or production costs. The benefit-cost analyst, however, is concerned with the social value of all goods and services produced or foregone regardless of the financial transactions involved. This parallel between benefit-cost analysis and profitability analysis is important both for the similarities and the differences. Profitability analysis and benefit-cost analysis are similar in the way the basic values are manipulated and compared once they have been measured. They are different in the things that are chosen for measurement and to some extent in the way things are measured. These differences will be made clear as the discussion progresses. Benefit-cost analysis is a tool for making decisions about the efficient use of resources. Therefore, it is proper to take into account, for example, the value of reductions in pollution damages or the value of increases in the recreational services provided at free public beaches even though neither will result in actual revenues. By the same token, the cost of using unemployed laborers should be zero in a social benefit-cost analysis, even though in order to hire the workers financial remuneration will be necessary. Therefore, while benefit-cost analysis can show what is being lost or gained by society as the result of a project, its estimates of benefits cannot be used, without modification, as estimates of revenues to be earned by the project nor can social costs necessarily be used as estimates of the money that government or firms will have to spend on the project.

Benefit-Cost Analysis and Other Decision-making Tools

Now that we know in greater detail what benefit-cost analysis is, we can specify more completely how it relates to other types of decision analysis. The first comparison may appear trivial, but considering the abuses and misinterpretations of benefit-cost analysis it is well worth discussing. Benefit-cost analysis is not a matter of just adding up all of the effects of a project and labeling all those that appear good as benefits and those that appear bad as costs. This can result in counting things that do not properly belong, in double counting of others, and sometimes in misspecifications so that a cost becomes a benefit or vice versa. Nor is it the mere recording of the financial transactions of the project. Benefits do not always result in revenues nor can all dollar outlays be considered a social cost.

As noted above, benefit-cost analysis is designed primarily to study the efficiency implications of projects. There are, of course, many other aspects that must be considered such as political acceptability, legality, and income-distributional effects. It is usually necessary for policymakers to take all of these aspects into consideration. A study that attempts to encompass all of these diverse aspects can be referred to as a general policy analysis. For the most part, benefit-cost analysis and policy analysis should be considered as two different types of analyses.

To say that economic efficiency is not the only item that must be considered by policymakers is not to say that benefit-cost analysis should be adapted or changed to consider all other aspects relevant to decisionmakers. Such a change would only decrease its ability to present information on economic efficiency effects. Efficiency is not the only thing of importance to policymakers, but it certainly is important and it does provide an excellent starting point for comparing trade-offs in the other aspects. For example, while individuals may feel that certain types of redistributions of income are desirable even if they must be achieved at the expense of efficiency, there is some limit to which they would be willing to push their argument. By keeping their attention focused on efficiency aspects, but also recording the distributional aspects of various projects, economists are able to demonstrate exactly what must be given up in terms of efficiency in order to achieve specified redistributional goals. The main thing to remember in this regard is that benefit-cost analysis is a very useful tool that has a sound theoretical basis, but it is a tool for primarily studying economic efficiency. To be disappointed because it focuses mainly on efficiency is to ignore its purpose, and to modify it by changing crucial definitions will produce a measure whose interpretation is dubious at the expense of the opportunity to consider efficiency. This is not to say that the distributional aspects of a project should be ignored. Just the contrary is true. But it is to say that efficiency aspects should neither be ignored nor distorted. Much of the information necessary to describe distributional effects can easily be collected in the process of doing a benefit-cost analysis. When this is the case, it is wholly appropriate to include it in the context of a benefit-cost report. This means that one section of the report would contain information on the net change in the value of goods and services produced and another would show which segments of the population reaped the benefits and which bore the costs.

There are two types of decision analysis that are economic in nature, yet that differ from benefit-cost analysis and therefore merit some consideration at this point. One of these tools is economic-impact analysis. Its purpose is to show the total economic effects of reallocations of resources. It is broader in scope than a benefit-cost analysis in that it considers every conceivable economic variable that might be affected, including tax revenues, public service requirements, income transfers, and so on. Another type, which is actually a subset of benefit-cost analysis, is called cost-effectiveness analysis. It is useful when it has been decided to achieve certain benefits and the only criterion is to obtain them at the lowest possible cost, where cost is defined as above. Both types of analysis are related to benefit-cost analysis, but they serve different purposes. An economic-impact analysis would be appropriate to describe the economic effects on government, business, and consumers of a major change, such as the introduction of a large company or government installation. A cost-effectiveness analysis is appropriate if it has already been determined that a certain project of a certain size is worth doing, and the only concern is to undertake the project as inexpensively as possible. Cost-effectiveness studies are often used in a military setting, such as in determining the least-cost way of obtaining a 99 percent effective missile detection system.

2 Measuring Benefits and Costs

The purpose of this chapter is to move from the theoretical basis presented above to the actual measurement of benefits and costs. Before doing so, however, it will be necessary to lay a little more groundwork. The first section discusses the problem of selecting the proper frame of reference while the second compares two basic approaches open to the benefit-cost analyst. The basic tools for measuring benefits and costs are the demand and supply curves. Accordingly, the third section will focus on their interpretation and use in benefit-cost analysis. The final section describes in detail some of the problems of using demand and supply curves in a practical analysis and suggests ways of overcoming them.

General Frame of Reference

It should be clear by now that the main purpose of a benefit-cost analysis is to determine whether the net value of goods and services produced rises or falls when a specific project (reallocation of resources) is undertaken. Before taking up specific identification or measurement issues, however, there are some general points that should be emphasized.

The first point concerns the *accounting stance* that is used as the basis for a particular benefit-cost analysis. The accounting stance issue revolves around the question: should a benefit-cost analysis describe the change in the value of output for the world or for just some part of it, for example, a nation, region, state, or city?

Many things must be considered when selecting an accounting stance. From an accounting point of view, it is evident that the more general the stance taken, the higher will be the cost of performing the study. Therefore, if it is obvious from the outset that most of the benefits and costs will accrue to a specific area, little harm will be done by appropriately confining the analysis. This strategy will result in a final measurement of benefits and costs that will be incomplete but the conclusions to be drawn about whether to approve the project will probably not be affected. After all, the purpose of benefit-cost analysis is to provide useful information to decisionmakers, not necessarily to make absolutely accurate measurements of every effect. It is simply inefficient to continue refining the measurements of a project's effects unless the benefits of the improved information are worth the cost.

19

From a political and institutional point of view, government decisionmakers are likely to be primarily concerned with the welfare effects on members of their constituency. The implications the project may have for people in other parts of the country will often be of secondary importance. Bearing these points in mind, the following recommendations can be made. The accounting stance that should be taken is the smallest one that includes all of the significant benefits and costs. In most cases this can be fairly easily determined by a preliminary listing of the expected outputs of the projects. From a practical point of view, the accounting stance should probably be consistent with the interests of the governmental decisionmakers who will use the results of the study in arriving at a decision. For example, if national economic efficiency is an important goal, then the appropriate accounting stance would be that of the nation overall rather than that of a region or state.

Once the accounting stance has been determined, the basic question to ask is how the nation (or a specified part of it) will be affected by the project under consideration. Ideally, the resolution of this question involves a description of the expected outputs of the project and a determination of how valuable those outputs will be to society. It is important to keep in mind that this analysis involves a "with-without" comparison rather than a "before-after" comparison. That is, we are interested in determining the value of output without the project and comparing that estimate with a measure of the value of output with the project. A before-after comparison is logically inappropriate because it may result in benefits or costs being attributed to the project when, in fact, those effects would have occurred in any event. For example, expansion of an existing highway may lower the cost of transportation thus providing cost savings to existing users and benefits to new users. It is obvious that road use will increase over time as population grows and as new plants, homes, and marketing centers are built. The goal of a benefit-cost analysis of the road improvement is to separate out the increase in production due to the new road (with-without) from those due to other reasons such as population growth that would have occurred anyway.

Two Basic Approaches

According to one view, the proper methodology for a benefit-cost analysis involves the identification and measurement of all gains and losses caused by a project. We can refer to this methodology as the *general equilibrium approach*. That is, with the reallocation of resources necessary to implement the project, there are some individuals who will gain and some who will lose. Drawing upon Mishan's (1975) discussion, the benefits of a project are the maximum that all gainers would be willing to pay for the advantages offered by the project. The costs are the minimum amount the losers would have to be compensated in order to keep them at the same level of welfare they enjoyed prior to the project. It should be clear that this definition of benefits and costs follows directly from the Hicks-Kaldor criterion for assessing improvements in social welfare (see the above discussion). If the amount that potentially could be collected (the benefits) is greater than the amount necessary to compensate the losers (the costs) it is obvious that the losers could be completely compensated with enough left over to make at least one person in the economy better off.

An alternative, though related, approach is to measure benefits as the total willingness to pay by all individuals for the *direct outputs* of the project. Similarly, costs would be measured by the total amount individuals would be willing to pay for the goods and services that could be rendered if the resources to be employed by the project were instead used in their next highest valued use. This approach is referred to as the *partial equilibrium* (or *direct output*) *approach.*

The main difference between these two approaches is that the partial equilibrium approach focuses attention solely on the direct effects of the project while the general equilibrium approach considers all effects whether directly or indirectly related to the project. Under most circumstances, however, the two will provide the same substantive information; yet, the latter will involve substantially less work and be less subject to misinterpretation.

This difference can be explained by referring back to the example used in chapter 1. Recall that when the project was announced the boat rental company stated its intentions to move to the new lake. Using the general equilibrium approach, the gainers and the losers from this would have to be identified and the values they place on such a move would have to be measured. Since the firm indicated that it would make the same profits in either case, the only gainers and losers would be the consumers in the two locations. The gainers would be the consumers at the new location. The amount they would be willing to pay for this indirect effect of the project depends upon the value they place on the services provided by the rental boats. The losers would be the consumers at the old location and the amount they stand to lose depends upon the value they place on the boat rental services. However, unless there is some reason to believe that the consumers in the two different areas are different, these two amounts will cancel out. Therefore, when adding up the total benefits and costs, these indirect effects of equal absolute size but opposite sign will have no effect on the net gain in the value of goods and services produced. Using the partial equilibrium approach, the effect of the relocation of the boat renting operation would not even have been considered because it is not a direct output of the project.

The cost of using the partial equilibrium approach is less than that of using the general equilibrium approach because the former requires consideration of fewer effects than the latter. (This savings may not appear significant in the context of our example, but in actual studies it can be quite large.) At the same time, if for example the effects of the boat rental firm do cancel out, the less expensive partial equilibrium approach will provide results identical to those of the general equilibrium approach. We will return to this point shortly.

The discussion concerning these two approaches is somewhat clouded by the many different adjectives used to modify the words benefits and costs. For instance, there are direct benefits, real benefits, intangible benefits, and pecuniary benefits. It will be useful, therefore, to more clearly define many of these different types of benefits and costs and to show their interrelationships before continuing on with this comparison. A schematic to be used as the basis for this discussion is found in figure 2-1.

Any project will result in a number of effects that can usefully be broken down into two main categories: direct effects and secondary effects. The former are the effects that result from the goods and services that are directly produced by the project. These direct effects are the benefits as measured by willingness to pay for the direct outputs and the costs of producing the direct output measured in terms of foregone production. Secondary effects are the changes in the value of production (both increases and decreases) generated indirectly by the project.

Both direct and secondary effects can be divided into tangible and intangible components. The difference between these is the relative ease with which values can be appraised in monetary units. Viewing this distinction in terms of polar cases, tangible effects are relatively easy to value in dollar terms whereas

SOCIAL BENEFIT = DIRECT BENEFITS PLUS NON-CANCELLING SECONDARY BENEFITS

SOCIAL COST = DIRECT COSTS PLUS NON-CANCELLING SECONDARY COSTS

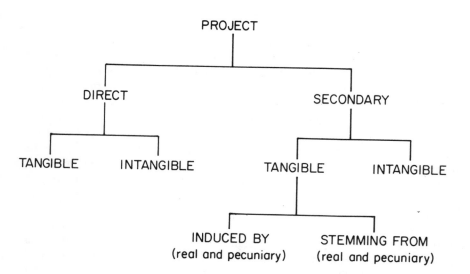

Figure 2-1. Categorization of Effects of Projects

intangible effects are not susceptible to being valued in dollar terms. It is important of course to realize that ease of measurement will change over time as data sources and economic methodologies are improved so intangible effects may ultimately become tangible. Often discussions of benefit-cost analysis get mired down in a controversy over whether intangible effects should be included in an analysis. This is really not a relevant issue. All of the outputs of a project that positively or negatively affect people's welfare should, in principle, be taken into account in a benefit-cost analysis. The relevant question, therefore, is not whether these things should be part of a benefit-cost analysis, but rather how can they be included in a meaningful way. At the very least, the intangible effects should be identified in the benefit-cost study and, where feasible, estimates of the physical magnitudes involved should be provided.

A final categorization involves the separation of tangible secondary effects into *induced-by* and *stemming-from* secondary effects. Stemming-from effects refer to increased output that stems from the output of the project. As a simple example, suppose that one of the outputs of a dam project is water for irrigation. This water can be used to produce wheat which is then used to produce flour which is used to produce bread. Everything except the irrigation water is a stemming-from secondary effect. From an economic point of view, it should be noted that if all these various effects were counted as direct benefits, total willingness to pay would be overestimated. This overstatement occurs because the value of the water is a component of the value of the wheat, which, in turn, is a component of the value of the flour, which, in turn, is a component of the value of bread. Taking the willingness to pay for all of these items will count the value of water four times. In addition, it will also count the value of wheat three times and the value of flour twice. In order to avoid this multiple counting of benefits, it is necessary to concentrate attention only on the direct output of the project and find the willingness to pay for water.

To look at this problem another way, note that even if the output of wheat, flour, and bread rises as a result of the dam, this increased production occurs only if other inputs besides the additional water are allocated to their production. Therefore, when there is full employment of productive resources, output in other parts of the economy must decrease. In the context of the irrigation example, the increased value of wheat, flour, and bread over and above that added by the extra water will be matched by an equal decrease in value of output elsewhere.

An induced-by secondary effect is the extra value of production that occurs as a result of the demands induced by the monetary payments generated by a project. For example, if a project is built in a certain area, during the construction phase and to a lesser extent during its operation, payments will necessarily be made to individuals and businesses for services rendered. These payments will, in turn, result in extra expenditures on everything from wine and cheese to education and operas. Therefore, output of these products will increase, However, this increase can only occur if there is a decrease in output elsewhere (if the assumption of full employment is granted). The gains in these areas are canceled out by losses in others. Therefore, except under the conditions noted below, these stemming-from and induced-by secondary effects will have no net effect on the total value of output.

We must also note that both of these secondary effects can be broken down into real and pecuniary effects. Pecuniary effects are those that deal with money prices and costs rather than with the real opportunity cost of foregone output or the real benefits of an actual increase in output. An example of a pecuniary secondary effect is provided by the case of a hotel on a particularly favorable spot on a lake whose water quality would be improved by a pollution control project. The cleaner water would more than likely increase the demand for the hotel's rooms, which would mean that the proprietor could increase his rates. This gain to the hotel owner, however, is exactly offset by an equal loss to individuals who use the hotel. There has been no change in the actual cost of producing hotel services. The only change that has occurred is a transfer of income from hotel users to the owner due to the scarcity value of the hotel.

If the hotel owner increases the number of rooms in the hotel, the cost of doing so is a real cost to the economy but here again it would be matched by the increase in the value of hotel services. In this situation there would be pecuniary effects (the extra payments for the original rooms; gains to the owner and losses to users) and stemming-from secondary effects (the additional value of services provided by the new rooms which is matched by a decrease in the value of output elsewhere). The net result of both effects is, of course, no change in the total value of goods and services produced.

Bearing the above discussion in mind, the distinction between the general and partial equilibrium approaches should now be clear. The partial equilibrium approach focuses only on the left-hand side of figure 2-1 while the general equilibrium approach considers both sides of the figure. In instances where the secondary effects cancel out, the two approaches yield identical results. However, there are cases where the secondary effects do not cancel out. The most frequently cited of such cases are unemployment and secondary external or spillover effects such as pollution. (See the later section on externalities for a more detailed discussion of external effects.) If there are unemployed resources or differences in employment conditions among areas, secondary benefits may not result in a zero net effect on the value of production. If a project is built in an area with high unemployment, the indirect expansion of output would not necessarily result in a decrease in production elsewhere. Therefore, since the goal of benefit-cost analysis is to find the net increase in the value of goods and services produced, such increases in production should be counted as a real benefit of a project.

The existence of secondary external effects can also cause the results of the two approaches to differ. As an example, suppose that an indirect effect of a project is the construction of a petroleum refinery. The value of the oil is essentially the same regardless of the area of the country in which it is refined. However, the increase in oil production will necessarily be accompanied by an increase in the amount of waste products pumped into the air. The exact amount of damage produced, however, will not necessarily be the same regardless of the location of the plant. Rather, it depends upon climatic and other environmental factors, the relative location of other productive and consumption activities, and population distribution and density. It is obvious that all of these determinants are site sensitive and so secondary external effects will not necessarily cancel out. Building a plant in one area and causing a certain amount of pollution damage will not guarantee that an equal amount of damage will be prevented by transferring the resources necessary to build and operate the plant from other uses.

A final difference between the two approaches is that even when all secondary effects cancel out, the general equilibrium approach provides a complete picture of the income distributional effects of a project. Frequently, policymakers are as concerned with who is gaining and who is losing as they are with the overall magnitudes of the gains achieved. In such instances, the general equilibrium approach should be used in order to provide the relevant information about income-distributional effects to policymakers.

The primary goal of a benefit-cost analysis is to show a project's net effect on the value of output. In order to accomplish this objective, it is necessary to identify and measure the social benefits and costs of the project. Social benefits are expressed as the sum of the direct benefits plus any noncanceling secondary benefits. Similarly social costs are the sum of direct costs plus any noncanceling secondary costs. As a practical guide to obtaining a measure of social benefits and costs, it is recommended that the partial equilibrium approach be adopted as the basic methodology because it will generally achieve the desired results and yet is easier to perform than the general equilibrium analysis. In cases where it is believed that secondary effects will not cancel out and there is reason to believe that the difference in the results of partial and general equilibrium analyses will be significant, the analysis should be appropriately expanded. This can only be determined by a careful study of all potential effects. Therefore, the general equilibrium approach will be useful during the premeasurement phase of a study, while the partial equilibrium approach should be used as much as possible during measurement.

Demand and Supply

The Demand Curve and Consumers' Surplus

The basic tool used by economists to measure willingness to pay for goods or services is the demand curve. There are many things that affect the amount of any good a person will purchase per period of time, and these include its price, the prices of other goods, and the income and tastes of the individual. A demand curve describes how quantity purchased per period varies due to changes in price only. That is, a demand curve reveals the relationship between the amounts of a certain good that will be purchased per period of time at various prices with all other relevant variables such as income, tastes, and the prices of other goods held constant. To illustrate these points, we refer to the demand curve for product X in figure 2-2, which measures the price of X along the vertical axis and the quantity per time period along the horizontal axis. At prices of $10, $8, and $6 the quantities demanded per period of time will be 6, 7, and 9, respectively. If the price were to fall, for example, from $10 to $8—but everything else that

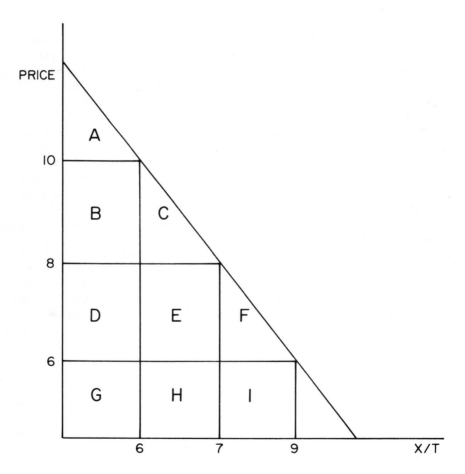

Figure 2-2. The Demand Curve and Consumers' Surplus

could affect demand remains the same—quantity demanded would increase from 6 to 7.

The effect on the demand curve of changes in the other parameters can be represented by changes in its shape and position. For example, if there is a change in consumer taste such that good X becomes relatively more desirable, the entire demand curve will shift to the right indicating that more will be purchased at every price. Changes in the prices of other goods can also have an effect on the location of the demand curve. For example, a rise in the price of sausage will shift the demand curve for ham to the right (as people substitute ham for sausage), but may shift the demand curve for eggs to the left (as less sausage is consumed, the demand for eggs may fall). Income can affect market demand curves in two ways. For most goods the higher the income, the larger will be the quantity demanded at each price. However, for some goods (for example, inexpensive meat), as income rises demand will fall as people substitute better quality items. The distribution of income can also be important. For instance, if a considerable part of a country's wealth and purchasing power is in the hands of a relatively small percentage of the population, the demand curve for luxury goods such as diamonds and expensive cars will be much larger than would be the case were income distributed more equally.

In summary, demand curves show how willingness to pay for various items varies with the amount demanded per period, provided other important determinants of demand are held constant. Conceptually each individual, or perhaps family unit, will have a demand curve to represent its willingness to pay for all goods and services. This statement does not mean however that they each purchase some of all goods because the amount demanded at any non-negative price may be zero.

Most goods in an economy are *private goods,* which means that consumption by one person or family precludes consumption by others. For instance, a loaf of bread is a private good that, once consumed by one family, is no longer available for consumption by others. In principle, we can find society's willingness to pay for a private good by horizontally adding the demand curves of all of the relevant individuals. That is, we can obtain the total or market demand curve for a commodity by adding the various quantities that individuals would purchase at each price. For example, if at a price of $4, only three individuals desire to purchase good X and they do so at the rate of 10, 15, 18, respectively, then the total quantity demanded at $4 is 43. To obtain a complete market demand curve, this horizontal sum (all quantities at each price) would have to be taken at all prices.

In contrast to private goods, *public goods* can (in the extreme case) be consumed equally by everyone in the relevant geographic region. One person's use or consumption of a public good does not exclude others from using it also. National defense, police protection, radio and television broadcasts, and uncongested highways are examples of items entailing substantial public-good characteristics. Public goods are relevant to the benefit-cost analyst because many services provided by government agencies are of this nature. Total willingness to pay for such goods can, in princple, be found through a vertical summation of the demand curves of individuals. That is, since one person's consumption of a public good is not affected by others' consumption, total willingness to pay for each unit can be thought of as the sum of each individual's willingness to pay for a given amount of it. For example, if three individuals are willing to pay $4, $7, and $18, respectively, for 20 units of public good Y then total willingness to pay for the 20 units is $29. Because good Y can be jointly consumed, the willingness to pay of all potential consumers must be considered. To obtain a complete market demand curve, this vertical sum will have to be taken at all levels of output. In the analysis that follows we will always, unless otherwise indicated, be using total or market demand curves—horizontal summation of individual demand curves for private goods and vertical summation for public goods.

Given the distribution of income and the structure of society's tastes, demand curves can be used as a measure of willingness to pay for various amounts of the good per period of time. For example, in figure 2-2 if there are seven units available per period of time, the market price will be $8. Market price, however, is only a measure of what consumers have to pay on the market, it is not a measure of their total willingness to pay. Note that if the amount on the market were only six, some people would be willing to pay up to $10 rather than do without the product. Consequently, at a price of $8, such consumers are getting a bonus of at least $2, because they are able to purchase the good for a price less than they would be willing to pay. The total amount of this bonus is referred to as *consumers' surplus,* and when price is $8 it can be represented by the sum of areas *A, B,* and *C* in figure 2-2. That is, consumers' surplus is the difference between what all purchasers would be willing to pay for a particular amount of the good rather than do without it and the amount they actually have to pay on the market. (To be precise, the correct measure of consumers' surplus is the relevant area under the *income compensated* demand curve which takes into account the effect a change in price has on real income. This effect is likely to be small except in the case of large price changes for commodities that take up a large percentage of total expenditures, and so for practical purposes it can often be ignored.)

The Supply Curve and Producers' Surplus

An important tool used by economists in the measurement of social costs is the supply curve. A supply curve shows the amounts of a good that will be produced per period at various prices, other things equal. There are many things that can affect the quantity of a good supplied during a period, including the prices of inputs, the state of technology, the entrepreneurial ability of producers, as well as the selling price. The supply curve, however, concentrates on selling price, holding other influences constant. An example of a supply curve is provided in figure 2-3. If the market price is $5, 10 units will be produced each period; however, if the market price were to increase to $7, and all other potential influences on supply remained constant, quantity produced would increase to 14 units per period.

The supply curve of an individual competitive firm is its marginal cost curve. Marginal cost is defined as the additional cost, including a normal profit, incurred by the firm in order to increase output by one unit. This curve is upward

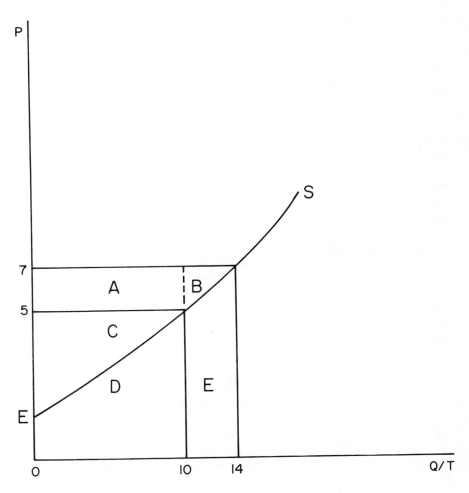

Figure 2-3. The Supply Curve and Producers' Surplus

sloping even when the unit cost of inputs remains constant due to the decrease in productivity as extra inputs are used with fixed equipment. (Microeconomics texts refer to this relationship as the law of diminishing marginal productivity. A full scale discussion of this law and its relationship to upward sloping marginal cost curves is beyond the scope of this book. For interested readers unfamiliar with basic economic analysis, it is suggested that they refer to any elementary economics text for a more complete discussion.)

To illustrate the link between marginal costs of production and quantity supplied, let us assume that the curve pictured in figure 2-3 is a marginal cost curve. That is, it shows the extra cost involved in producing extra units of output. Now, suppose that the price facing the firm is $7 per unit. It will maximize profits if it produces 14 units per period. Why is this so? Notice that at any level of output less than 14, the marginal cost of production is less than the extra revenue ($7 per unit) achieved by producing and selling one more unit of output. As long as total revenue increases by more than total cost as output expands (that is, as long as marginal revenue exceeds marginal costs) the firm will find it profitable to continue expanding output. Notice, however, that if output is expanded beyond 14 units, marginal cost is greater than the $7 selling price. Therefore, it would not be profitable to expand output beyond 14 units because at that point costs begin to increase faster than revenue, and profits will start to fall. At a price of $7 per unit profits increase as output is expanded toward 14 units and decrease as output goes beyond 14 units. Therefore, profits are maximized at exactly 14 units of output. The analysis is identical for other prices. Regardless of the price, profit is maximized for the competitive firm by operating where price equals marginal cost. Therefore, the marginal cost curve is the supply curve of the competitive firm.

Analogous to the relationship between individual and market demand curves, the market supply curve for an industry is the sum of the supply curves of the individual firms in that industry. In the short run the supply curve is the sum of the marginal cost curves of the firms currently in the industry. When this type of short-run curve is applicable, the supply curve can be used to obtain a measure of producers' surplus (that is, actual revenue over and above the revenue that would have been necessary to get the output produced). Since the supply curve is the marginal cost curve, total cost of production can be measured by the area under that curve. For example, in figure 2-3, the total cost of producing 10 units of output is equal to area D. The first unit of output costs approximately $1 to produce, the second slightly more than that, and finally the tenth unit costs $5 to produce. To find the total cost we must add all these amounts, which is the area under the curve up to 10 units of output. This amount will be produced at a price of $5 per unit and the resultant total revenue can be represented by the areas $C + D$. The difference between total revenue and total cost is called *producers' surplus*. It is represented by area C. Using these concepts we can see that if quantity produced were to increase from 10 to 14, total cost (including normal profits) would increase by an amount equal to area E and producers' surplus would rise by $A + B$.

In the long run, when there is time for firms to enter or leave a competitive industry due to increases or decreases in price and profit, the concept of producers' surplus is no longer applicable. In this longer time period, the market supply curve is not the sum of the supply curves of the individual firms but rather a description of how costs in the individual firms will be affected by the entry of firms. For example, if entry has no effect on production costs the long-run supply curve will be perfectly horizontal. In the short run an increase in price will encourage existing firms to expand output according to their marginal cost curve, but this increase in price will encourage the entry of new firms eager to take advantage of the economic profits made possible by the higher price. This entry will drive prices down as more firms attempt to sell more output. A new equilibrium will be reached when prices are pushed down to the point where entry is stopped, which will be at the original price—assuming that there have been no changes in production costs for the individual firms. In this case, increases in demand will be met in the long run by equal increases in quantity supplied at the existing price.

In cases where the entry of firms cause the production costs of individual firms to rise (for example, because of increased pressure on prices of productive inputs), then the long-run supply curve will be upward sloping. The entry of firms will stop before the price is pushed back to its original level because a higher price will be necessary to cover the increased production costs. Therefore, at any point on the long-run supply curve, the dollar amount represents the marginal cost of producing the last unit in each firm; in addition, it is also the average or unit cost of producing each level of output up to that point. In the case of the upward sloping long-run supply curve, an increase in industry output increases not only marginal cost of production, but also the unit cost of production on all preceding units of output.

Total cost at any level of output must be represented differently in the case of long-run supply. For example, if the curve in figure 2-3 is a long-run supply curve, at 10 units of output total cost is $50; that is, the $5 average unit cost times the 10 units of output. This amount is represented by the area $C + D$. Since the total revenue gained from selling 10 units is also represented by the area $C + D$ there is no producers' surplus in the long run. The total cost of increasing output in the long run from 10 to 14 must also take into account the increase in costs of producing the original 10 units of output. The cost of producing the 10th through the 14th units is $E + B$, but as a result of the expansion of industry output, the cost of producing the first 10 units will increase by an amount equal to area A.

Demand, Supply, and Market Equilibrium

A market equilibrium price and quantity of output can be determined using demand and supply curves. Consider demand and supply curves D_1 and S respectively in figure 2-4. The market will achieve an equilibrium—a point from which

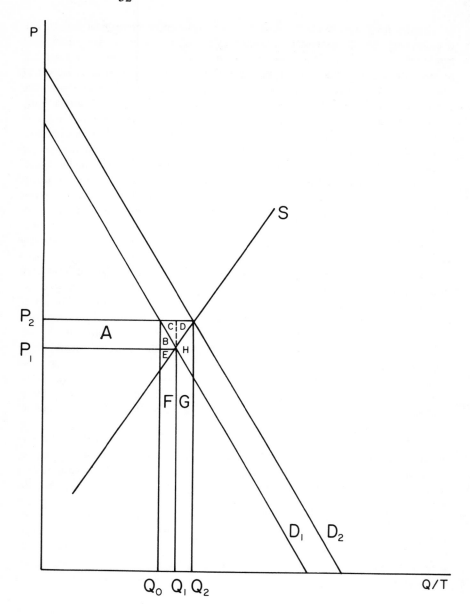

Figure 2–4. Demand and Supply and Measures of Willingness to Pay

there is no tendency to change, other things equal—at a price of P_1 and an output level of Q_1. At any higher price the quantity supplied will be greater than quantity demanded and price will tend to fall because producers could not sell all they produced at that price. At prices below P_1, quantity demanded will be greater than quantity supplied and so prices will tend to rise. Only at P_1 and Q_1 will the amount that producers are willing to sell just equal the amount consumers are willing to purchase.

There is an important interpretation that can be placed on this output-price combination. Recall that demand measures willingness to pay for a good or service and that supply measures the marginal cost of production. Two important conclusions follow. First, given the assumptions behind this analysis, the proper amount of this good is being produced, because the last unit produced has a value equal to the social cost of production (that is, the value of foregone alternatives). Second, in benefit-cost analyses market prices are the correct measure of willingness to pay for small increments in production whereas information about demand and supply curves is necessary to provide correct estimates of willingness to pay for nonmarginal changes in output. This last point is the subject of the next two sections.

Use of Demand Curves in Benefit-Cost Analysis

Although the discussion of demand curves and consumers' surplus has been quite succinct, it should be clear that if we have measures of the relevant demand curves it is possible to place the correct value on outputs of proposed projects. In cases where the project will result in only a marginal change in the output of the good in question, it is not even necessary to know the shape of the entire demand curve. The downward slope of the demand curve indicates that the only way that more of a certain good can be sold in a given period is for its price to fall. But if the increase in output is quite small relative to the existing quantity already passing through the market, then it is reasonable to assume that the extra amount will have virtually no effect on price; therefore, if the existing market price is known, it can be used to value new production because it is the willingness to pay for existing output (on the margin).

When the change in production is nonmarginal, the problem becomes more complex. This complexity can be illustrated with the aid of figure 2-2. Assume that a project increases production of good X from 6 to 9, thus resulting in a fall in market price from \$10 to \$6. The amount that consumers actually pay for these additional three units is \$18 (\$6 each); this amount provides a lower-bound estimate of consumers' willingness to pay for the additional output. However, as a result of the increase in output, there has also been a gain in consumers' surplus of $B + C + D + E + F$. This increase in consumers' surplus is the sum of the consumers' surplus gains associated with the existing purchases ($B + D$, or $24) and those gains associated with the increased purchases ($C + E + F$).

Originally, six units were sold at a price of $10 but, with the increase in output, these units are now sold for $6 each. Therefore, the purchasers of these units would be willing to pay up to $24 to have the project undertaken because this is the amount they stand to benefit because of the reduction in prices. The consumers' surplus arising from the additional output is the amount the new purchasers that enter the market would be willing to pay over and above the $18 they actually have to pay rather than go without the product. Assuming that the demand curve is essentially linear, the area of this triangle can be obtained by taking one half of the product of the (absolute-valued) change in quantity times the (absolute-valued) change in price, that is, $.5(4 \times \$3) = \$6$. In summary, if there is a nonmarginal change in output as a result of a project, the gross benefits are the amount paid for the new production plus the increase in consumers' surplus for new and existing consumers.

As a final note, the actual importance of consumers' surplus in practical analysis may have been overemphasized in the foregoing discussion. This is not to say that it is not theoretically correct nor that it should not be used when relevant. We would argue just the opposite. We have spent more time discussing the problems of measuring benefits when there are nonmarginal changes because it is a somewhat more difficult concept to explain. However, many benefit-cost analyses can probably be adequately performed by looking only at marginal changes, so it is only necessary to look at market prices.

Use of Supply Curves in Benefit-Cost Analysis

Using the complete demand and supply analysis it is possible to define appropriate measures of costs. To do so, it is necessary to consider the markets for the various productive inputs utilized by the project. If the amount of an input to be used is small relative to total supply (so that the project does not affect the input's price), the existing market price for the input is the proper measure of the value of foregone production. This follows directly from the definition of a supply curve as the sum of the marginal cost curves of the firms in the industry and from the discussion of the meaning of the equilibrium market price. In most cases, a project's demand for inputs will be small relative to the available supply; thus, it can often be safely assumed that the existing input prices provide appropriate measures of opportunity cost.

However, when there is a nonmarginal change in the demand for inputs it will be necessary to allow for any resulting change in the prices of inputs. Let the difference between the demand curves D_1 and D_2 in figure 2-4 be the additional amount of a representative input that will be purchased at each price if the project is undertaken. In the event that the project is approved, the equilibrium price and quantity produced of this input would increase from P_1 and Q_1 to P_2 and Q_2, respectively. In addition, the amount purchased by the original consumers would fall to Q_0. The difference between Q_0 and Q_2 is the quantity of the input employed by the project. The fact that the input to be used on the project comes from new production and from transfers from current users is quite important; it is necessary to find the foregone production that results from each effect. As will be emphasized in the following discussions, the opportunity cost of using a productive input may well depend upon the source of that productive input.

A useful approach to discussing opportunity costs of inputs is to first identify their actual dollar cost to the project and then show how that dollar outlay must be modified to arrive at a measure of true opportunity costs. The presence of the producers' surplus will affect the results, so we must consider cases in which producers' surplus is, and is not, relevant. Let us consider first a situation involving producers' surplus. In this case we must modify the actual dollar or budgetary cost of a project by adding the loss in consumers' surplus to original users and subtracting the increase in producers' surplus. This consumers' surplus loss represents a true social cost while producers' surplus gain is a mere transfer from consumers and taxpayers to producers involving no net social costs or benefits. In terms of figure 2-4, these amounts and their sum can be represented as follows:

$$
\begin{array}{lll}
& \text{Actual budgetary cost} & = C+B+E+F+D+H+G \\
+ & \text{Decrease in consumers' surplus} & = A+B \\
- & \text{Increase in producers' surplus} & = -A-B-C-D \\
\hline
& \text{True opportunity cost} & = B+E+F+H+G.
\end{array}
$$

In the short run when there is a producers' surplus, the true opportunity cost of an input is equal to the actual dollar cost of that input minus that part of producers' surplus not canceled out by the loss in consumers' surplus.

In the long run when there is no producers' surplus, there is no transfer gain to producers that must be subtracted from budgetary costs to arrive at an estimate of the social costs of an input. Therefore, the true opportunity cost of an input is the dollar budgetary outlay plus the loss in consumers' surplus. In terms of figure 2-4, this amount will be equal to $A + 2B + C + D + E + F + G + H$. The fact that area B is counted twice may appear paradoxical and, thus, deserves further explanation. It is counted once as the consumers' surplus loss to the original consumers of the input and again as part of the increased cost of producing those inputs used by the original consumers. We are arguing on the one hand that the original users suffer a social cost as a result of input prices rising, while on the other hand society suffers a social cost as a result of the opportunity cost of providing those inputs rising. These effects are separate and distinct and must both be counted in order to obtain a proper measure of social cost.

As indicated earlier, producers' surplus is only relevant when we are considering a short-run supply curve. Therefore if the shift in the demand curve for the inputs will be a one-time thing during those periods when construction is taking place, it is highly likely that there will be a producers' surplus. On the other hand, if we are talking about long-term or permanent changes in the demand for an input (for example, because the input will be used throughout the life of the project), then a long-run supply curve is appropriate and producers' surplus will not be relevant. These comments should be borne in mind in the discussions that follow.

Summary Comments

For the case of well-functioning competitive markets, we have discussed the main elements of benefit-cost analysis. We can summarize these points as follows. In the case of marginal changes, either in the outputs provided by the project or in the demand for project inputs, existing market prices provide the appropriate measures of social benefits and social costs. In the case of non-marginal changes, it is necessary to take account of any resulting changes in market prices and, thus, any changes in consumers' or producers' surplus.

However, the benefit-cost analyst is usually confronted with the task of evaluating programs or projects involving complexities not adequately handled by the framework of well-functioning competitive markets. As mentioned above, it will sometimes be necessary to take a closer look at secondary effects to determine whether they cancel out. More importantly, properly interpreting demand curves is often a very difficult task. The reasons for this difficulty can be ascribed to three somewhat interrelated causes: (1) the existence of market distortions mean that special interpretations will have to be placed on market demand curves; (2) there is often less-than-complete information on demand curves; and (3) the existence of nonmarket goods poses special problems in the conceptualization and measurement of demand curves. The remainder of this chapter discusses each of these problems in detail and provides suggested methodologies for solving these problems. It should be remembered, however, that in each case the basic approach is to try to come up with an estimate of the proper demand curve to measure willingness to pay.

Prior to this more detailed analysis of special problems in benefit-cost analysis, some general observations are in order. First, there are some aspects of benefit-cost analysis that are simply beyond the scope of this book and probably beyond the competence of most noneconomists. For example, the actual econometric estimation of demand and supply curves falls into this category. For the economist-reader this restriction should pose no great problem. For the noneconomist, we can only suggest that a professional economist be consulted where more sophisticated economics (or econometrics) is required than that presented here.

The rest of this chapter deals with how to handle particular problems that may arise from time to time. But it is necessary to keep this discussion in perspective. Every benefit-cost analysis will not need adjustments for each of the problem areas cited. It will often be the case that most of these problems simply do not arise to any significant degree. If a problem has the potential for affecting the estimates of benefits or costs by relatively minor amounts, it can probably be safely ignored. Or if the problem is more significant, but there are insufficient time, data, or resources to properly handle it, it will only be possible to show that benefits or costs may be overestimated or underestimated and perhaps to indicate a range for the magnitudes involved.

Problems of Market Distortion

In this section the effects that market distortions can have on the estimation of benefits and costs are discussed. It will be convenient to divide most of these subsections into three parts: (1) a description of the distortion, (2) a discussion of how to measure costs when an input of a project is produced in a market with a particular distortion, and (3) a discussion of how to measure benefits if the output of a project is produced in a market with that distortion.

Monopoly

Firms that are the sole supplier of a particular good or service are called monopolists. Unlike the competitive firm, a monopolist has the power to set market price. The price selected by the monopolist will determine the quantity that demanders will be willing to take off the market. Presumably, the monopolist will select that price and level of output that will maximize profits. However, the fact that the monopolist has some control over price will lead to an inefficient level of output. To see this point, consider the demand curve (labeled D_1) and the marginal cost curve (labeled MC) in figure 2-5. The curve labeled MR_1 is the marginal revenue curve associated with D_1. The marginal revenue curve measures the change in revenue when output is increased by one unit. Since monopolists face the entire market demand, they cannot sell extra units unless they lower the price. Therefore, marginal revenue is always less than price at any level of output because price must be lowered not only for the last unit sold but for all previous units as well. The marginal revenue curve is important to the monopolist because by relating it to marginal cost the monopolist can

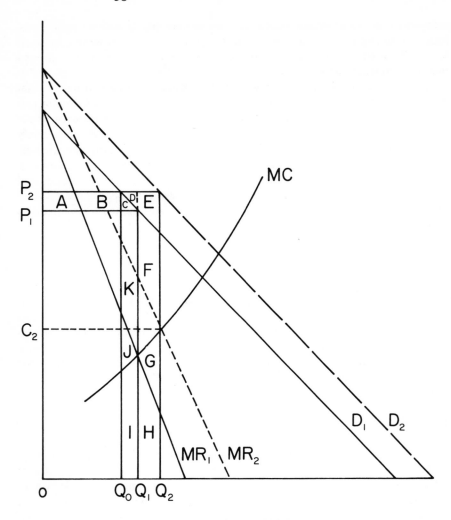

Figure 2-5. Monopoly and Willingness to Pay

determine the profit-maximizing level of output. If marginal revenue is greater than marginal cost, the profit-maximizing monopolist will expand output, whereas output will be reduced if the reverse is true. The monopolist will operate where MR_1 intersects MC and will produce Q_1 units of output and sell at a price of P_1. At this profit-maximizing level of output, price is greater than marginal cost. Therefore, we can infer from our earlier discussions that it would be socially beneficial to expand output beyond that provided by the monopolist because the amount society is willing to pay for extra units of this good is greater than the value of lost output (as measured by marginal cost) that results from such an expansion.

Cost of inputs produced by a monopolist. When materials purchased for a project are produced by a monopolist (or any firm with the market power to set price above marginal cost), market price cannot always be used as an estimate of the value of production foregone because of the difference between price and marginal cost. To be precise, the actual cost to society—that is, the willingness to pay for foregone alternatives—depends upon whether the inputs the project uses are newly produced or are taken away from current users. In the first case, the correct measure of social cost is the extra cost of supplying those inputs, not the purchase price that must be paid due to the monopoly power of the producer. In the second case, the proper measure is the price paid by the existing users because that is the monetary evaluation of the loss they will suffer from not being able to purchase the inputs any longer at their original price.

Nonmarginal changes will cause both new production and transfers from current users, so the total dollar outlay will have to be properly modified to account for both. This point can be demonstrated in figure 2-5. Let D_2 and MR_2 represent the new demand and marginal revenue curves for an input given that the project is to be undertaken. The new marginal revenue curve intersects the original marginal cost curve at Q_2, where with the new demand curve, the new profit-maximizing price will be P_2. Total revenue to the monopolist will increase from P_1 times Q_1 to P_2 times Q_2; this increase is represented in the graph as areas $A + B + C + D + E + F + G + H$ (letters refer to areas bounded by solid lines). The increase in production cost is represented by area $G + H$, which means that if we subtract $G + H$ from the area representing the revenue increase, we will have the increase in profits that result from the extra demand associated with the project. This extra profit is equivalent to the increase in producers' surplus discussed above, except that here it is also a long-run phenomenon because, by definition, there is no entry to a monopolistic industry. At the new price the amount consumed by the original consumers falls to Q_0. Therefore, it can be seen that the project will use $Q_0 Q_2$ units of the input, of which $Q_0 Q_1$ will be transferred from existing users and $Q_1 Q_2$ will be the result of new production.

In order to obtain an estimate of the true opportunity cost of using the inputs, we must add the loss in consumers' surplus and subtract the increase in monopoly profits from the dollar budgetary outlay to actually purchase the inputs. This amount can be represented as follows:

Actual budgetary cost	$= C + D + E + F + G + H + I + J + K$
+ Loss in consumer surplus	$= A + B + C$
− Increase in monopoly profit	$= -A - B - C - D - E - F$
True opportunity cost	$= C + K + J + I + H + G.$

Therefore, in those instances where a purchase from a monopolist will significantly affect the monopolist's demand, then it will be necessary to have information on the demand and supply curve. Some notion of the production costs of the monopolist may allow for a rough estimate of the increase in monopoly profit. In cases where neither curve is known, a useful approximation technique is to value all of the newly produced products at the marginal cost of producing the last one and to value the output taken away from consumers at the original market price. As can be seen from figure 2-5, the former involves an overestimate and the latter involves an underestimate; therefore, the measurement errors associated with this technique may tend to cancel each other out.

Benefits of outputs in an otherwise monopolistic industry. If the output of a project is produced in an industry that is a monopoly prior to the development of the project, the extra output should be valued by looking at the demand curve only and ignoring the production costs of the monopolist. The exact value of the extra output will depend on whether the change is marginal or nonmarginal. If the additional output involves a marginal change, then it can correctly be valued at the existing market price. However, if it involves a nonmarginal change in output, then it must be valued taking into account the gain in consumers' surplus that occurs.

Taxes

When excise or production taxes are placed on commodities, they drive a wedge between the cost to the producer and the price that the consumer has to pay. In these cases, special attention is necessary to insure that proper values are placed on goods produced by the project or on inputs used in its construction or operation. We can illustrate this point in figure 2-6. In this graph, the curve labeled S is a normal supply curve representing the marginal cost of production while S_t represents a supply curve that additionally takes into account taxes on production. The vertical difference between the curves is the increase in price at each level of output that the producer will require to operate in the presence of the tax. For instance at Q_2, the actual social cost of production is C_2 but the producer will not find it profitable to operate unless the price is equal to P_2.

Measuring opportunity cost when inputs are produced with production taxes. As in the case of monopoly, the proper measure of value for inputs will depend upon whether they are the result of new production or the result of transfers from other producers or consumers. To the extent that the inputs come from marginal increases in production, the supply cost represents the proper measure of social cost. If the inputs come from marginal reductions in the quantity used by other demanders, then it is proper to use the selling price as a measure of

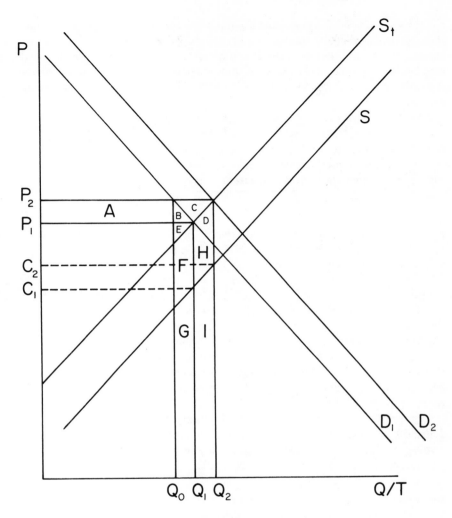

Figure 2-6. Taxes and Willingness to Pay

social cost. When there is a nonmarginal change in input demand, it is necessary to take into account both effects. Let D_2 and D_1 in figure 2-6 be the usual demand curves for this product with and without the project. Without the project, Q_1 units will be sold each period at a price of P_1. However, cost is C_1 and the difference between cost and price is the tax per unit. The project changes equilibrium quantity, price, and cost to Q_2, P_2, and C_2, respectively. The amount purchased by the project will be Q_0Q_2 of which Q_1Q_2 represents new production. To fully account for the opportunity cost of foregone production we must make the usual modifications for consumers' and producers' surplus, but in addition we must also subtract out the taxes paid on the newly supplied inputs. The taxes must be subtracted because they do not represent foregone production elsewhere in the economy. This amount can be represented as:

Actual budgetary cost	$= B + E + F + G + C + D + H + I$
+ Loss in consumers' surplus	$= A + B$
− Increase in producers' surplus	$= -A - B - C$
− Tax payments on new production	$= -H - D$
True opportunity cost	$= B + E + F + G + I.$

If producers' surplus is not relevant (that is, if the long run is the period of analysis), then the opportunity cost is $A + 2B + C + E + F + G + I$. The reason why area B is counted twice is explained above.

One question that may arise is why do we not subtract out all of the tax payments that are a part of the total cost outlay? That is, why is area F in figure 2-6 not subtracted out as well as areas H and D? The answers go back to the basic point that the opportunity cost depends upon where the inputs actually come from. Since the total willingness to pay of the original consumers of the $Q_0 Q_1$ units is represented by the relevant area under the demand curve, or $B + E + F + G$, this full amount must be included as part of opportunity cost because it is this willingness to pay that is the opportunity cost of transferring these inputs to the project.

In practical applications it will be necessary to have some notion of the demand curve and enough information on production costs and the time period involved to determine whether producers' surplus is relevant and to estimate that part of average costs attributable to tax payments.

Measuring benefits when outputs are produced in markets subject to production taxes. The analysis for measuring benefits in the presence of taxes draws on the same principles. In figure 2-6, consider the equilibrium generated by the demand curve D_1 and the supply curve S_t. The equilibrium price or marginal willingness to pay is P_1 even though the cost of production is only C_1. Small increases in production will then be valued by consumers at P_1. It may only cost C_1 to produce them, but the fact still remains that because of the tax, the willingness to pay is greater than production costs. As long as the tax is expected to be permanent, the correct analysis will use P_1 as the starting point in measuring the value of increases in output. It should be recognized that the reason willingness to pay is higher than existing costs of production is the result of the distortion caused by the tax.

In the event that there are nonmarginal changes in market outputs as a result of the project, we must go further than just using P_1. Obviously, if market price is pushed down as a result of a project, the increases in consumers' surplus must be included in the measure of benefits. On the other hand, to the extent that the new output is matched by reductions in output elsewhere in the economy, then the proper measure of benefits is the value of the increase in production made possible by the project. This benefit can be measured by using the supply curve net of taxes. We can ignore willingness to pay on the part of the consumers since their welfare has not really changed in this instance. They will be consuming the same amount as before; the only difference is that the output will be produced by a different source. The gains from the project stem from the fact that production can increase elsewhere. (For instance, see the case of the ferry in the example cited above.)

Subsidies

Subsidies are the opposite of taxes. Where taxes on production force consumers to pay more than the marginal unit cost of production for each unit that they purchase, a subsidy allows them to pay less than the marginal cost. Since subsidies are essentially the opposite of taxes this analysis is quite similar to the analysis of taxes and we should be able to proceed rapidly. The important thing to remember is that in the presence of a subsidy, there is a wedge between the cost of producing an item and the amount that people actually pay for it. Therefore, in evaluating costs of inputs or the benefits of outputs, this difference must be considered.

Consider figure 2-7. The supply curve S is the normal supply curve and S_s indicates the amounts that will be supplied with a subsidy. The vertical difference equals the per-unit subsidy. The interpretation of the downward shift in the market supply curve is that the producers can afford to charge consumers less at every level of output because what they do not earn in sales revenue will be made up in subsidy payments from the government. For example, at Q_1 the actual cost of production is C_1, but with the subsidy, producers can operate at a price of P_1.

Measuring opportunity cost if inputs are produced with production subsidies. In order to obtain a proper measure of opportunity cost in the presence of production subsidies it is necessary to make the usual modifications to dollar budgetary outlay and to add the amount of the subsidy on the new output. The subsidy must be included because it hides part of the real cost of production. The following graphical analysis of the subsidy problem is simplified by recognizing that producers' surplus can be measured in figure 2-7 either by area $L + M + N + E'$ or by area $A + B + C + D + E$. Note also that area E' is equal to area E. Bearing

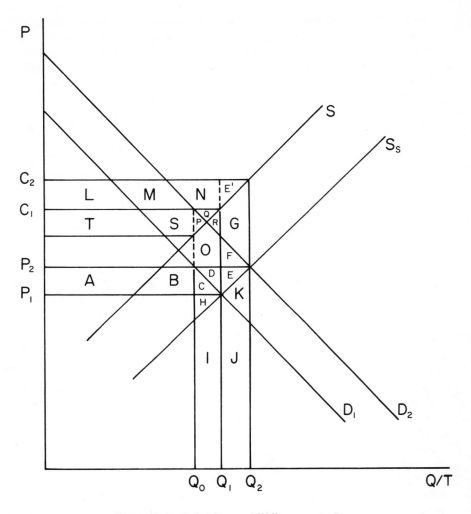

Figure 2-7. Subsidies and Willingness to Pay

these points in mind real opportunity cost can be represented in the following way:

Actual budgetary cost	=	$D + C + H + I + E + K + J$
+ Decrease in consumers' surplus	=	$A + B + C$
− Increase in producers' surplus	=	$-A - B - C - D - E$
+ Subsidy in new production	=	$E + F + G$
True opportunity cost	=	$C + H + I + K + J + E + F + G.$

In the absence of producers' surplus, real opportunity cost becomes $A + B + 2C + D + H + I + K + J + 2E + F + G$. The reasons for double counting area C have been explained above, but perhaps a few words are necessary regarding the double counting of area E. When it is recalled that E is identical with E', it is easy to explain why it is counted twice. The cost of the new production when there is no producers' surplus is equal to $E' + G + F + E + K + J$. By including E twice we are essentially just adding in E'. The reason it does not come in naturally is the substitution we made above in measuring producers' surplus.

For practical applications we need to know the same sort of information as in the case of taxes, except we will also need an estimate of how much the subsidy actually reduces the selling price.

Measuring benefits when outputs are produced in markets subject to subsidies. If the output of a project is produced in a market that is currently subsidized, extra units should be valued at what people will pay for them. However, if the project completely replaces or reduces the output of a subsidized firm or industry, the proper measure of benefits is the value of the resource savings made possible by the project. The former involves measurements along the demand curve, while the latter involves measurements along the unsubsidized supply curve.

For example, if D_1 in figure 2-7 is the market demand curve for the output of our project and the planned increase in output is Q_1Q_2, the total willingness to pay for this additional output is equal to area J. On the other hand, if the planned output is Q_0Q_1 and it will replace existing output, the net benefit will be $O + R + C + D + H + I$ if there is a producers' surplus. It will also include $P + Q + S + T$ when there is no producers' surplus.

Price Ceilings

Price ceilings are government decrees that the price for a certain item may not go higher than some predetermined maximum. Two well-known examples are rent ceilings and foreign exchange controls. Although these controls are subject to much controversy (and sometimes may cause as many problems as they solve) they do exist and as such can make it difficult to measure costs and benefits. In figure 2-8 if P_1 is the regulated price ceiling, the maximum that will be supplied is Q_1. Note however that at this price consumers will wish to purchase Q_2 units; that is, there will be excess demand for this good or service. Note that at the Q_1 level of output, willingness to pay is actually P_2 which is greater than the price that must be paid given the ceiling. This difference is the key to the proper measurement of costs and benefits.

Measuring costs when inputs are subject to price ceilings. If an input to be used on a project is purchased in a market subject to price ceilings, production of the input will not increase because suppliers are already producing all they care to at the constrained price. Therefore, all inputs used on the project, provided they can be obtained in a market with excess demand, must be transferred from other uses in the economy. Therefore, the opportunity cost of such inputs is the willingness to pay of the previous users. If the amount used is quite small relative to the total output, then P_2 is the appropriate measure of opportunity costs. For

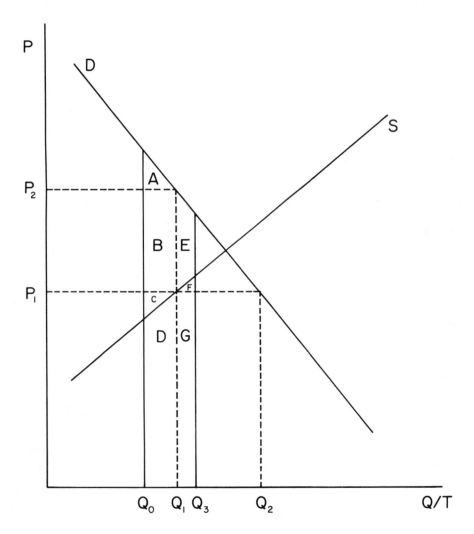

Figure 2-8. Price Ceilings and Willingness to Pay

larger amounts, losses in consumers' surplus must also be considered. For example, if the project were to use Q_0Q_1 units, then the opportunity cost is area $A + B + C + D$. Area $C + D$ is the total budgetary cost, while area $A + B$ is the loss in consumers' surplus to the original users of the input. Area B is the loss in consumers' surplus that would not be accounted for by using the price ceiling P_1 as a measure of willingness to pay rather than P_2. Area A is the loss in consumers' surplus due to the nonmarginal change.

Practical applications will require an estimate of the position of the demand curve at the constrained level of output. When one is not currently available, rough estimates may be possible if there are informal black markets due to the excess demand or if there is a notion of the value of the marginal product of this input when it is used in other industries.

Measurement of benefits when outputs are subject to price ceilings. Marginal changes in output should be valued at P_2 even though the existing market price is P_1. Benefit measurement with nonmarginal changes is analogous to earlier discussions; that is, we must account for changes in consumers' surplus. For example, if the extra output produced by the project is Q_1Q_3, the willingness to pay for it will be equal to area $E + F + G$.

Price Floors

Price floors are minimum prices mandated by a government or by some group (for example, a labor union, that has some degree of market power). The most common examples are minimum-wage laws, union contracts, and price floors for certain agricultural commodities. The analysis of this market distortion is similar to that of price ceilings, but there are a few elements that make it somewhat more complex. Consider the demand and supply curves in figure 2-9. Assume that a price floor of P_1 exists in this market. Note that at this price only Q_1 units will be demanded but suppliers will be willing to sell Q_2 units. Therefore, something will have to be done with the excess supply of Q_1Q_2. In the case of labor markets, for example, transactions completed below the fixed price will have to be prevented. That is, even though more workers are willing to work at P_1 than actually can find jobs, and what is more important, some would be willing to work at lower wages than P_1, an effective wage floor must prevent this undercutting from occurring. In the example of price floors on agricultural commodities the government will have to stand ready to purchase any excess supply.

Measuring costs when inputs are subject to price floors. The general analysis here is the same as the analysis of the above mentioned distortions. The proper measure depends upon whether the inputs come from additional production or

48

whether the inputs are transferred from other uses. The real problem, of course, comes in measuring new production when there is an excess supply. If we are talking about, say, an agricultural product selling at the fixed floor price of P_1, then Q_1 will be purchased by consumers. In addition Q_1Q_2 will have to be purchased by a government and either stored, destroyed, or perhaps disposed of in

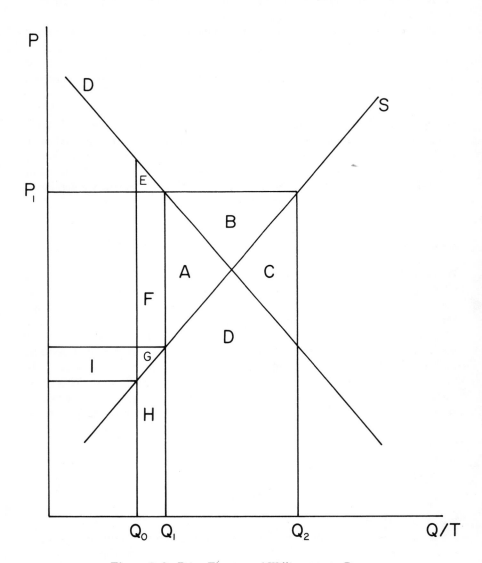

Figure 2-9. Price Floors and Willingness to Pay

another government program. In this case, although the value to current market users is P_1, the cost to society of employing some of the excess supply depends upon what is being done with that excess supply. If it is being destroyed, for example, the opportunity cost of employing it in some project is zero. If the item is being stored indefinitely, society could even benefit by using up some of the excess supply in a government project, thereby saving on storage costs. If the excess supply were being used in some other types of activities, then the social value of those activities represent the opportunity cost of diverting those productive inputs into other uses.

In the event that the project will use more than the existing excess supply, the actual cost of producing any additional amount must be taken into account. Therefore, if output is expanded beyond Q_2 in figure 2-9, the starting point for cost measurement is P_1. The exact nature of the cost will depend upon the size of the increment beyond Q_2 and whether or not there is a producers' surplus.

The case of price ceilings in the labor market is somewhat different. Here if the control is effective, there is no excess production. Laborers are merely prevented from moving into a particular field of endeavor. Therefore, while the actual cost of using this labor will be lower than the fixed market wage, it will not be zero. Rather, because the supply curve represents labor's opportunity cost in its next best use (including leisure) it is the proper measure of value. Therefore, in figure 2-9 while the dollar outlay necessary to hire the increase in labor Q_1Q_2 is $A + B + C + D$, the social opportunity cost of doing so is only $C + D$. We will talk more about the problems of measuring labor cost in the section on unemployment.

From the above discussion, it is clear that practical applications would require knowledge of what use is being made of any surplus production that would be used as an input in a project.

Measuring benefits when outputs are produced subject to price floors. The analysis of the measurement of benefits when there are price floors is apparent from the above discussion. If the price floor arrangement is expected to continue, the value of any extra output is zero or negative. At the fixed price, consumers are purchasing all they desire, and so any additional production will simply involve the government in further purchases of the excess supply. If the project replaces existing producers, the benefit will be the net value gained by releasing the inputs those producers previously used. (See the later section on measuring benefits when outputs are subject to quantity control.)

Quantity Controls

Quantity controls are very similar to price floors. However, rather than preventing price from falling by prohibiting transactions below a certain price or by standing ready to purchase any surplus at a stated price, the desired price is maintained by preventing quantity from expanding beyond the appropriate level. Refer back to figure 2-9. If output is kept from expanding beyond Q_1, the market price will remain at P_1. Note that P_1 is above the price where demand intersects supply. Consequently, in the absence of output control, production would tend to expand and price would tend to fall.

Measuring costs when inputs are subject to quantity controls. If the quantity control is binding, the inputs used on the project will be transferred from other uses. In this sense output controls are similar to price ceilings. Therefore, if it is a marginal amount, the unit value of the inputs is P_1. If the use of the inputs involves nonmarginal effects on the market, then the analyst must consider consumers' surplus. For example, the true opportunity cost of using $Q_0 Q_1$ units in a project would be $E + F + G + H$.

Measuring benefits when outputs are subject to quantity control. There will be no benefits for extra production if the control prohibits their use. If, however, the output of a project replaces production elsewhere, the benefit is the value of the resources released from production in that market. This information is available from the supply curve. For example, if the project produces $Q_0 Q_1$, the benefits will be H if the industry outputs are produced with a producers' surplus and $H + G + I$ if they are not.

Unemployment

To the extent that resources used on a project would not otherwise be producing something of value, the opportunity cost of using them is zero. That is, society would not be giving up anything to achieve the increase in production brought about by the project. Therefore, in times of unemployment, it may often be necessary to correct the dollar wage bill to arrive at a proper measure of the social opportunity cost of labor.

In deciding how many units of any type of labor to hire, firms must compare the value of that labor's marginal product with the current wage. The value of the marginal product is the amount of extra output produced times the existing market price for that output. In a competitive economy the wage paid to any worker will equal the value of that worker's marginal product. If one firm is not willing to pay workers their marginal product others will, so competition in the labor market will force this equality between a worker's wage and marginal product. In these circumstances if we know the wage of a worker, we also know the value of that worker's marginal product, which of course is a perfect measure of the value of what will be lost if the worker is used in another activity.

In many cases, however, modern economies suffer unemployment due to a lack of sufficient aggregate demand or regional immobility of workers. Sometimes the unemployment is a short-run phenomenon, but, as in the case of the Great Depression or the unemployment problem in Appalachia, it is a chronic problem. Of course, even when unemployment does occur, it never involves the entire labor force and seldom ever an entire labor type. When there is unemployment, the wage rate necessary to hire a worker—although it does represent a cost on a financial ledger—is not an accurate measure of the value of the marginal product foregone.

In order to correct for this problem, it is necessary to estimate the percentage of the workers employed by the project that will be drawn from the ranks of the unemployed. If it is estimated, for example, that 20 percent of the workers would otherwise have been unemployed, then only 80 percent of the wage bill can be used as an estimate of the value of foregone production. Haveman and Krutilla (1968) have done extensive research on specifying which types of labor are used in different types of projects and have developed an approach using national unemployment figures to estimate the percentage hired that would have previously been unemployed. It is beyond the scope of this book to provide an extensive review of their analysis, but it would be very useful reading prior to performing a benefit-cost analysis when it is known that there will be considerable unemployment involved.

It is also important in these cases to take into account the fact that unemployment rates may change over time. Therefore, if the project will take several years to complete, it is best to consider how the percentage of unemployed workers used in the project will change over the life of the project. Just because there is 20 percent unemployment of the workers involved at the time the project is started does not mean that it will necessarily remain at that level.

There are at least two other considerations regarding unemployment that should be considered. The first is the psychic income from labor and the second is how to handle unemployed capital equipment. With regard to psychic income, labor is a peculiar input in that it is impossible to separate its use from its ownership. An individual does not sell his services in the same manner he would rent a summer cottage or sell the mineral rights to a piece of land. He cannot separate himself from the transaction and as a result, in addition to the monetary gains, he must also suffer the boredom from or distaste for a particular type of activity or, on the other hand, enjoy the satisfaction of seeing a job well done or engaging in an activity that he particularly enjoys. If a strict interpretation of the changes in the value of output that results from a project is used, proper attention must be paid to these gains and losses. In principle, the output provided by a worker includes the positive and negative services he produces for himself. Thus, if you hire an unemployed individual you may not reduce the value of market production but you may reduce the amount of leisure enjoyed by that individual. In this case, the opportunity cost of employing an otherwise unemployed person is technically the value of the foregone leisure. By the same token, if an individual has an absolute hatred of idleness, especially in relation to the particular type of work needed by the project, he or she may be willing to pay a certain amount out of savings for the privilege of obtaining such a job. In that case, the opportunity cost would actually be negative. The same general analysis applies when individuals are transferred from one type of work to another. If the types of work afford different amounts of personal satisfaction to the workers that are not corrected for by differences in wages, then the opportunity cost of labor should in principle be modified appropriately.

Although there has been some work done on estimating positive and negative psychic income, it is preliminary and often difficult to apply. This lack of an existing methodology makes practical application of these theoretic considerations quite difficult. However, this should not cause serious problems unless a project affects the lifestyles of many individual workers. For almost all practical applications, the benefit-cost analyst can safely ignore this theoretic nicety.

The problem of the unemployment of capital equipment is identical as far as the concept of opportunity cost is involved, but practical problems in measurement can arise. If a piece of otherwise unemployed capital equipment is used on a project, the value of foregone production is properly measured at zero (assuming the depreciation rate is unaffected by use). For example, if a truck would become obsolete in five years regardless of how much it was used and if it would otherwise be idle, its opportunity cost is zero. To the extent that depreciation is related to usage rather than time, there is an opportunity cost involved because by using capital equipment now its use in the future is reduced. A key difference between capital and labor arises in connection with the conservation of productive capacity. If a worker does not work now, there is no way unused effort can be shifted to the future. Often, however, a machine has only a certain amount of productive capacity and not using some of it in the present will make it available for use in the future. The opportunity cost of using it now is the foregone value of future services.

Government and Business Transfer Payments

A problem that is often linked to unemployment is how should changes in unemployment compensation payments be handled in a benefit-cost analysis. For example, if, as the result of a project, certain individuals who were formerly collecting unemployment compensation are given the opportunity to work, government or business unemployment payments to them will cease. This problem can be dealt with very easily. Unemployment compensation payments should be ignored as far as efficiency aspects are concerned. These are, as their name indicates, merely transfers from one group to another; consequently, they can be ignored by the benefit-cost analyst (unless such payments are of interest for their distributional impacts).

Externalities

Another type of market distortion that is pervasive in our economy is externalities. For our purposes, externalities can be defined as occurring when a firm or individual is not liable for all of the costs arising from its activities or when it is not fully compensated for all of the benefits it confers on others. An example of the first case is pollution. In the process of producing steel, for example, the producer also emits smoke and other undesirable by-products which impose costs on other individuals and firms. From an economic efficiency point of view, the total cost of producing the steel is the sum of the value of the resources expended on its production plus the value of output foregone because of the release of the waste products into the environment. Since the firm does not pay all of these costs, the production of steel is in a very real sense being subsidized. The market supply curve does not include all of the actual costs of production, and, consequently, lies below the true social supply curve. The difference between the social and the market supply curves does not arise because of payments received from a government as in the subsidy case described above; rather, these costs are borne by the people who are damaged by the pollutants. If we assume the curve labeled S_s in figure 2-7 represents the market supply curve of the industry and that the S curve represents the social supply curve including all production and environmental costs, the analysis of the measurement of costs is directly analogous to the above discussion of subsidies. The total dollar outlay for project *inputs* supplied under conditions involving negative externalities (for example, pollution) must be modified by the relevant changes in consumers' and producers' surplus as well as by the negative external cost associated with any increased supply of the input.

Any negative externalities that accompany the intended *output* of a project are best handled by treating them as a cost. For example, let the two supply curves S_2 and S_1 in figure 2-10 represent the social and private marginal cost curves, respectively, of producing the output of a project. That is, S_1 is the industry supply curve as we normally interpret it, whereas S_2 includes the external costs that the private producer does not pay. Therefore, area B represents the actual private cost of producing Q_1 units of output. However, the true opportunity cost of producing this amount is actually $A + B$ where A represents the social cost caused by the negative externality. It is this measure of the social cost of production ($A + B$) that should be used in a benefit-cost analysis.

The other type of externality occurs when a firm or individual is not fully compensated for the provision of desirable goods or services. An example of this

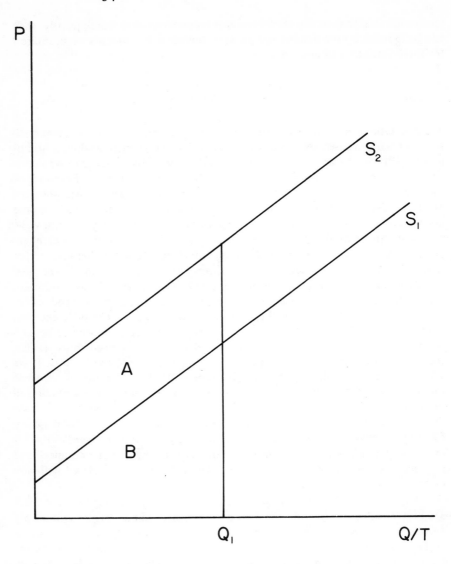

Figure 2-10. Externalities and Social Opportunity Cost

phenomenon is the beekeeper who can sell his honey, but cannot, in many instances, sell the pollination services performed by his bees. In this example, the net social cost of producing honey is lower than the cost suggested by the market supply curve by the value of the pollination services. This case can be represented in figure 2-6 where S_t represents the market supply curve and S the social cost curve. The analysis of measuring the opportunity costs of inputs with positive externalities is analogous to the case of taxes. The dollar outlay must be modified by the addition of consumers' surplus and the subtraction of producers' surplus, where applicable. In addition, the value of the positive externality must be subtracted from the cost of increased output.

The positive externalities that accompany the intended output of a project should be handled as a separate output. To properly include this effect in the analysis it is necessary to measure actual willingness to pay by constructing the demand curve for this positive externality.

Because of the similarity of externalities to taxes and subsidies, there is no need to go into further detail at this time. In the section on problems of no markets, however, we will consider in some detail the practical problems of measuring the social costs and benefits associated with certain types of externalities.

Problems of Less-Than-Complete Information

Cost-Savings Approach

In certain cases when there is not sufficient information to derive a demand curve per se, willingness to pay can be estimated by the cost savings made possible by the project. That is, as a result of certain public projects, private expenditures of individuals and firms are sometimes reduced. Construction of a bridge, for example, can eliminate or reduce the use of resources on longer more circuitous routes. Along the same line, modification of waterways can make them more navigable and, thus, reduce the cost of moving goods from one place to another. Also a dam can reduce flood hazards and water treatment plants can reduce damages from water pollution. An estimate of the savings that result are appropriate values to use in benefit-cost analysis because they represent a lower-bound estimate of the amount that individuals would be willing to pay rather than do without the project. This method was introduced in our discussion of the hypothetical project presented in chapter 1. In that case, the benefit of the transportation services of the dam to existing customers turned out to be equal to the actual cost of running the ferry they previously used. The case of improved navigation for instance, can be handled in the same manner. If the barge traffic made possible by a waterway project can carry existing cargo at a lower cost than the existing transportation mode, then the reduction in the real resource costs of using those alternative transportation modes represents a social benefit of the project.

Note that in neither of these examples was it necessary to estimate a demand curve for transportation. The rationale for this shortcut is that the overall social value of transportation services is not important per se, because the amount has not changed; rather, it is just being provided in a different (lower cost) manner. If there is no differential in willingness to pay for water versus rail transportation, as would be expected in the case of most industrial commodities, there is no need to consider transportation services per se.

The cost-saving methodology will be most accurate where the reduction in transportation cost will not induce a significant increase in the quantity of transportation services produced. For example, consider figure 2-2 again. Let the initial price and output be 10 and 6 respectively. Now, suppose that a government project reduces the cost of producing this output to 8. The benefits associated with the first 6 units of output is the cost savings as represented by area B. Note that at the new price, the quantity demanded increases to 7, and the gross willingness to pay is represented by areas $B + C + E + H$. Therefore, B will be an underestimate of benefits. However, if the demand curve is relatively steep, the amounts represented by areas $C + E + H$, will be quite small, so B will be a close approximation to total benefits. Even if the cost-savings method does underestimate benefits, the values obtained may provide useful order-of-magnitude estimates for decisionmakers.

Cost savings provided by flood protection and pollution control activities can be handled similarly. Without a flood control project, for example, a certain area will suffer a certain amount of losses each year, so the benefits of the project include the reduction in these losses. To demonstrate this point, it will prove useful to set up a general model. Assume that at the time the project is being considered annual flood protection costs are estimated to be some amount k. This estimate would include properly amortized increased costs of construction, expenses to keep sandbags ready, and so forth. With these protective activities the losses that will occur in the event of a flood are L. (To make the problem easier to discuss, we are only assuming two weather states, flood and no flood; in an actual study it would be necessary to use data on a variety of alternative weather states.) Therefore, if climatological records indicate that the probability of a flood occurring in any year is P, then the total expected cost to the area is:

$$k + PL.$$

The first term is the protection costs and the second is the average annual losses. The construction of the dam will normally not eliminate all of the damage caused by flooding. Let q_1 be the percentage of annual protection costs that are saved and q_2 be the percentage of losses that are avoided if the dam is built. Assuming all else remains the same, the expected total flood-related costs with the dam will be:

$$(1 - q_1)k + P(1 - q_2)L.$$

The savings that will result from the dam is the difference between costs *with and without* the project, that is, $q_1 k + Pq_2 L$. In other words, the benefits depend upon the probability of flooding, the percentage reduction in other protection costs and flood damages, and the actual amount of damages that would occur in the absence of the project. It is obvious then that the benefits from flood protection will vary depending upon the location of the project. In practical applications, then, it will be necessary to estimate k, P, L, q_1, and q_2.

There is an important element to keep in mind here. The amount of damages that occur in the absence of the project, L, is dependent upon the amount of resources devoted to other types of protection. As more protection activities are used, protection costs will go up but losses from flooding will decrease. From an efficiency point of view then, it would be optimal to use more protection activities as long as the increase in costs is less than the reduction in damage. It may be the case in an actual benefit-cost analysis that L is not at the optimal point; that is, it may be possible to reduce total expected costs by increasing k. In this event, a complete analysis should include an examination of the other types of protection activities. It may very well be that more savings can be obtained by doing something other than building a dam. If this is so, there will be an overestimate of benefits using the status quo in a cost-savings methodology. There may be certain institutional or sociological constraints on using these other methods, and, if so, the estimate of benefits will be correct given the constraints. The analyst is obligated to make the nature of these constraints explicit to the decisionmaker, however.

The same general points apply to a project that reduces pollution costs. Total costs are the sum of protective costs and the actual damage that results regardless of protection. An estimate of willingness to pay for the project would be the reduction in the sum of these two items for all affected entities, be they firms or individuals. Here again, it is possible that the optimum amount of protective activity is not being currently undertaken, and this fact will have to be considered to avoid overestimating benefits.

Comparative Products

Another method that is sometimes used to obtain estimates of benefits and costs when incomplete information about demand and supply curves is a problem is to use willingness to pay for comparative products. This is a rather simple procedure that can often provide very useful first approximations, but it is also easy to abuse. The easiest way to explain this technique is with the aid of an example. Assume that a certain product or service will be introduced to an area for the first time as a result of the project. If similar services or products are produced in other areas, it may be possible to use the market values there as an estimate of willingness to pay in the area under study. For example, in the case of a public campground, there may be a commercial campground in a similar area nearby and the admission fee there could be used as an estimate of the value of a recreation day provided by the project.

Along the same line, if a project results in the destruction of a recreational facility, it may be possible to obtain an estimate of the social costs by using information on a similar facility elsewhere.

There are a number of hazards involved with using this procedure, however. For one thing, these estimates ignore consumers' surplus, so they underestimate benefits. A more serious problem is that the areas to be compared must be essentially identical or the values derived will not be strictly comparable. This requirement means that population characteristics such as density, racial makeup, and income distribution should be essentially the same. In addition, the number of complement and substitute goods must be roughly the same. For example, if there are many other similar recreation sites in the area used for comparison, whereas in the area under study there are none, willingness to pay for an additional site would be higher (other things equal) in the latter area than in the former.

Problems of No Market

Value of Product as an Intermediate Good

In many cases where there are no formal markets for the products of public projects, the willingness to pay for such products can be estimated by studying the value created by the products. For instance, irrigation water is usually not sold per se, or at least seldom at prices that cover cost of production. However, its value can be determined by finding the effect of the extra water on consumers' and producers' surplus in various agricultural markets. Similarly, pollution abatement is an input into the production of certain products, and therefore the benefits of pollution abatement can be estimated from the market for the final goods. For example, industries that use water in the production process may enjoy some cost savings as the result of a water pollution control program. The use of this method should not be suspect due to the warning given above about double counting by using stemming-from secondary effects. This method estimates willingness to pay for an input by finding the value of its net productivity in its next use in the production line. There is no attempt to add all values through a production process to a final product. For example, the value of irrigation water to the wheat farmer is included by this method, but not the value to the flour or the bread manufacturer.

In some cases, all gains will accrue to consumers, but in others producers can benefit as well. Let us look at these two situations in terms of figure 2-11 where Q is a product which uses the output of a project as an intermediate good. That is, Q is produced using X, and X, which is not dealt with explicitly in the graph, is the output of the project under consideration. Assume that as a result

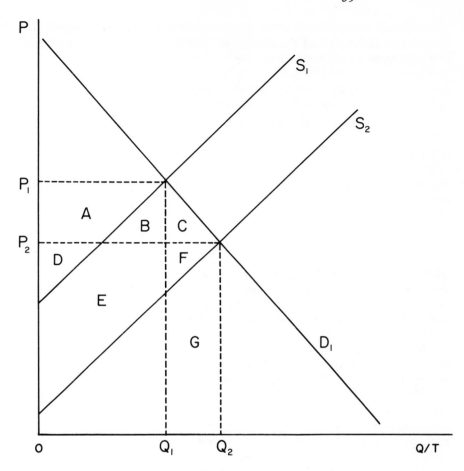

Figure 2-11. Intermediate Products and Willingness to Pay

of a project production costs of firms providing Q are reduced, thereby shifting the industry supply curve from S_1 to S_2. In cases where there is no producers' surplus (that is, the action results in a strict reduction in the cost of production for all units) the benefits fall completely on consumers and can be measured by the increase in consumers' surplus or area $A + B + C$. This is the net gain they receive because of the increase in production of Q that results because of the project. Note that the gross willingness to pay for the effects of the change in the supply curve of Q is $A + B + C + F + G$. But $F + G$ is the increased cost of producing the extra output of Q, and since it will not be included in our estimate of the cost of producing the output of the project, X, it must be subtracted to arrive at a correct measure of benefits.

The case where there is a producers' surplus is slightly more complicated; the net gain is the sum of the changes in consumers' and producers' surplus. From the graph we can see the following:

New producers' surplus	$= D + E + F$
$-$ Original producers' surplus	$= -A - D$
Net gain in producers' surplus	$= E + F - A.$

If we add this amount to the net increase in consumers' surplus, we obtain a total net gain of $B + C + E + F$. In practical applications, the net gain to producers can be estimated by the following expression for the change in profits that occur as a result of the project:

$$(P_2 Q_2 - \Sigma r_i^2 a_i^2) - (P_1 Q_1 - \Sigma r_i^1 a_i^1),$$

where the as represent the various inputs (including X), the rs the prices paid for them, and Σ is the common notational device for summation. The *super*scripts on each correspond to the *sub*scripts on the Ps and the Qs. That is, the amounts and types of other inputs as well as their prices may change as a result of the project (for instance, the producers may use less fertilizer with the extra water).

If there is no producers' surplus involved, then the change in revenues will be matched by an equal change in cost and so there will be no effect on producers. The net gain then is represented by the change in consumers' surplus.

The values derived using this method should be used with caution. For example, even if a project provides 1000 acre-feet of water per year and it is estimated that the extra value provided to producers and consumers of wheat is $2500, the benefit-cost analyst is not justified in using $2.50 as a unit valuation for the water. The $2500 indicates what is gained by producing the water, and the $2.50 is merely an average. It does not mean that benefits would increase by $250 if 100 more acre-feet of water were provided by the project.

Value of Time

When dealing with projects that are related to transportation services, the value of time saved is often a very important benefit. For example, the construction of a bridge, road, tunnel, airport, or even improved air traffic control systems, may decrease the amount of resources necessary to achieve a given movement of goods or people. In most cases this resource savings will be accompanied by a reduction in travel time. The social benefit of saving time is, of course, the amount that people are willing to pay for it. In part, this willingness to pay is based upon the dollar savings of moving materials from one point to another, but there is also the value that individuals place on the extra time made available which can now be allocated to other uses. We have already discussed methods of evaluating cost savings, but evaluating time savings is somewhat different because of the lack of an explicit market. There are two ways of attacking the problem. First, one can consider the net value of goods and services that could be produced in the extra time. Second, one can consider the value individuals place on time.

The first approach is the easier of the two but it is also subject to more qualifications. If we can assume that the wage an individual receives is approximately equal to the value of his or her marginal product (that is, the additional revenue arising from the sale of what that person produces), then the wage rate is the proper unit of value for time savings. If a subway system, for example, reduces travel time by a half hour for each of 100 workers who earn $3 an hour, then the value of extra production thus made possible is $150. There are fifty man-hours a week that can now be utilized in production and each man-hour is worth $3 on the margin. It is interesting to note that in the case of well-functioning labor markets, even if people are traveling during leisure hours, the wage rate provides the correct unit value of time. Individuals will work extra hours as long as the additional earnings compensate for the lost leisure time. Therefore, in a free, well-functioning market, the wage rate is also equal to the value of leisure time on the margin.

There are some drawbacks to this argument, however. If work has some disutility to the employee, then the wage rate overstates the value of leisure time. If there are other costs to the employer of hiring workers such as insurance, employment taxes, uniforms, and so on, then it will be an underestimate of the value of time. In the first instance, a worker will stop working extra hours when the marginal value of leisure is higher than the wage to allow for compensation for the dissatisfaction of work. In the second instance, if there are costs other than the wage in hiring each worker, the employer will stop hiring when the cost of doing so is equal to the value of the marginal product. Thus the value of the marginal product will be higher than the wage. Therefore, it will often be necessary to make adjustments to the wage rate before it can be used as a measure of the value of marginal product or of leisure time.

The potential problems with this method may be even more severe than the foregoing discussion suggests. For one thing, powerful firms or labor unions in either the input or the product markets may place a wedge between the wage rate and the value of the marginal product. Also in many cases, people may not be able to work as much or as little as they would like because of union restrictions, forty-hour-week laws or traditions, unemployment, or other constraints. Such problems in adjustment may prevent the wage rate from accurately measuring the social value of time (on the margin).

The second general method of estimating the value of time is to obtain a direct estimate by observing individual behavior. There are several ways to perform this estimation. While we discuss only two such methods, we consider the results of studies using other approaches. The basis for all of these methods is the actions of individuals who have a choice of several transportation modes such that they can reveal their preference for time savings versus extra cost. That is, by noting the differences in travel time and costs between two methods of travel it is possible to estimate the trade-off between time and cost savings. The nature of this comparison is as follows. If an individual chooses a particular mode that takes 30 minutes and costs 75 cents, when he has the option of another that takes 45 minutes but costs only 50 cents, he has demonstrated a willingness to pay of 25 cents to save 15 minutes in travel time.

One very simple method of using this information derived by Beesly (1965) and modified by Harrison and Quarmby (1969) is to plot these differences in travel time and cost on a four-quadrant diagram such as the one shown in figure 2-12. This figure shows the relationship between changes in travel time and changes in cost, with travel time changes being measured along the vertical axis and travel cost changes being measured along the horizontal axis. Each point on the graph represents the combination of time difference and cost difference for two alternative transportation modes for one person. Those points in the second quadrant represent individuals who are willing to give up time to save some money while the opposite holds true for points in the fourth quadrant. Individuals represented in the third quadrant do not really have much of a choice because the method they use is both cheaper and faster than any alternative. For normal commuting travel it is unlikely that there will be many points in the first quadrant because they would represent a choice that is both more expensive and slower than any alternative. (This phenomenon may occur in recreational travel, however, because travel may be an enjoyable part of the activity.)

An estimate of society's average trade-off between time and willingness to pay (as measured by cost savings) can be found by drawing a straight line through the origin such that the minimum possible number of points lie to the northeast of (or to the right and above) it. The slope of this line can then be used as an estimate of the trade-off between travel time and cost savings. In this hypothetical graph the trade-off is 25 cents per 10 minutes.

The justification for using this line is that it minimizes the number of people who are made to *appear* irrational by their choice of travel method given the trade-off value selected. At point *B*, the individual gives up something less than 10 minutes in order to save 25 cents, and given the estimated trade-off value this person has made a correct choice. Individual *A*, however, gives up more than 10 minutes to save the 25 cents. If the 25 cents to 10 minutes trade-off is the correct one this person should have chosen the alternative transportation method. This line is drawn such that it minimizes the number of points such as *A*. Obviously, this method is not perfect, but it can provide a useful approximation with little formal analysis. Using this method on British data, it has been estimated that the trade-off is somewhere between 30 percent and 50 percent of the wage rate for a comparable time period.

Another more rigorous way to use this information is to assess the relationship between cost and time differences with the aid of the following equation
using normal statistical procedures:

$$\Delta \text{ cost} = a + b \, \Delta \text{ time}.$$

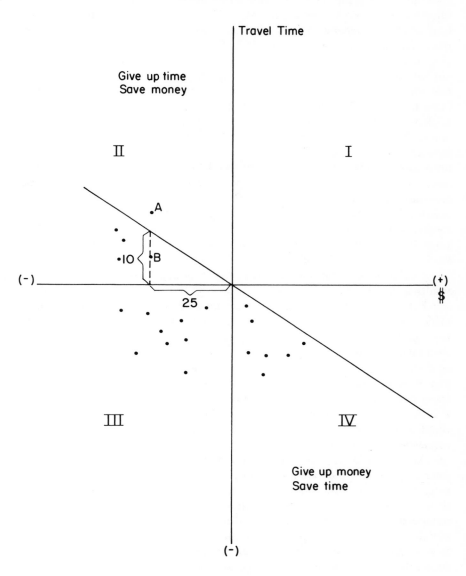

Figure 2–12. Determination of Value of Time

The *a* coefficient can be interpreted as a measure of inertia or psychic attachment to the chosen method of transportation, whereas the *b* coefficient can be interpreted as the trade-off value between time savings and cost savings. Using this method Hensher (1976) estimates that the average trade-off is 57 cents per hour (in 1971 prices). By using an expanded model he also found that the trade-off value varies according to trip length (the longer the trip the lower is the unit value placed on time saved), amount of time saved (the larger the amount of time saved, the higher is the average valued placed on it), and income (the higher the income of the individual involved, the higher the trade-off value).

There are other ways to use similar data to measure the value of time saved, but we cannot go into all of them here. The interested reader is referred to the references at the end of the book (for example, Beesley (1965), Goodwin (1976), Howe (1976), and Vickerman (1972)). It is interesting to note that most of these alternative techniques come up with trade-off values of somewhere between 25 percent and 50 percent of the wage rate. The consistency in these estimates is heartening because these values can be used to provide upper and lower bound estimates of the value of travel time savings. Trying to estimate a travel-time value for every separate benefit-cost study can be very expensive, and unless there is reason to believe that there is something unique about the individuals involved in a particular study, the final results will probably not be significantly improved by doing an independent study. For practical applications, it is recommended that estimates obtained from a simple wage rate analysis be modified by reducing them from 50 percent to 75 percent. This approach will provide a useful range of estimates that is in accord with existing empirical results.

Before concluding this section, there are a few more points that should be made. First, it is logical to assume that different values are placed on different types of travel time; savings in walking and waiting time may have higher values than savings in riding time. Therefore, it is important to specify the exact composition of travel time and how it will be changed by the project. In addition, it may be important to separate the willingness to pay for reductions in average travel time and reductions in the variance of travel time. People will often accept a longer average travel time in order to achieve a reduction in the variation in travel time because this will lower the probability of such things as missed travel connections or late appointments.

Another point is that in many instances very small time savings have no value at all even if they are achieved by a large number of individuals. There is often little that can be done with a small amount of extra time especially when there are other constraints on behavior. A thirty-second reduction in a five minute subway ride will likely be of little value. By the same token, a twenty-minute reduction in a transatlantic plane trip may offer relatively few benefits to travelers. This point is especially relevant in light of the other components of such a trip such as taxis to and from airports, waiting in line for tickets and customs, the time allowed to adjust for changes in time zones, and so on.

The point about the small time savings is not universally true, however, for we must allow for the breaking up of bottlenecks in a complex transportation system. Faster elevators in a subway may only save a few seconds in the trip but may allow for larger numbers of passengers to use a station without congestion and these effects would be felt throughout the system. It is this entire benefit, net of extra costs, that should be attributed to the elevators.

Value of Life and Health

The value of life and health must be included as a benefit or a cost of many projects in order to insure proper consideration of all gains and losses. For disease control projects improved health is the main benefit, and for flood control projects one of the expected benefits can be a reduced death and injury rate from floods. On the other hand, the construction and operation of certain projects may increase the probability of death or illness, and these effects, properly evaluated, should be included as a cost. Examples of such hazardous projects are nuclear power generating stations and manufacturing plants that release harmful elements into the environment.

Before we discuss methods for valuing life and limb, some introductory remarks are in order. Life and limb are generally perceived as being goods of infinite value. Nevertheless, in a world of scarce resources, it is often the case that hard choices have to be made concerning allocating resources to reducing the probability of illness, injury, or death as opposed to using them elsewhere in the economy. The objective of a benefit-cost analysis in such cases is to make sure that social willingness to pay for these decreased probabilities of death, injury, or illness is greater than that for the goods and services foregone to obtain those decreased probabilities. Notice that the question is posed in terms of probabilities. It is not useful to ask, for example, what would one be willing to pay to save one's own life. It is obvious that in virtually all cases, a person's willingness to pay to prevent certain death is limited only by his income or by limits on his capacity to earn income.

Projects involving improvements in health entail reductions in the probability that any one person will be injured, sickened, or killed. The result of disease control projects will be a reduction in mortality and morbidity rates. This means that each individual in society faces a lower probability of being affected by the disease. It is not possible to identify in advance those individuals who will avoid the disease. Similarly the cost of a nuclear power plant may include an increase in the probability of illness and death due to exposure to radioactivity. It will not be possible, however, to identify in advance who will be the unlucky ones to suffer. The proper measure for benefits from reduced mortality and morbidity rates is the willingness to pay to achieve those reductions while the social cost of increased morbidity and mortality rates is the amount that people would have to be paid to fully compensate them for those increases. It is not a matter of finding the value of a specific individual's life or health. Even in these probabilistic terms, the analysis may seem crass or materialistic, but it should be remembered that individuals make these kinds of choices all the time. They ride in automobiles rather than walk even though the probability of death or injurty is increased as a result of that choice. They are simply demonstrating that the value of the time saved is worth the increased probabilities of an accident.

Bearing these points in mind, we can now discuss an approach for measuring society's willingness to pay for reductions in the risks to life and limb. A useful way to consider this problem is to divide it into two parts, the production aspects and the individual evaluation aspects. The production aspects include the direct changes in output due to changes in mortality or morbidity rates. To be completely accurate this approach should include changes in the value of services provided by nonmarket work, the most notable example of which may be housework. In addition, this measure should include the changes in output that occur as resources are released due to decreased health care hazard-avoidance efforts. Taken together these items provide a fairly good measure of the output gains resulting from changes in the probability of death, injury, or illness. For example, in the case of decreased morbidity this measure would indicate how much more additional output society could expect partly as a result of having a healthier work force and partly as a result of expending fewer resources on health care and hazard avoidance. Of course, this measure represents only a part of what society would be willing to pay for a reduction in morbidity or mortality. It is a useful measure because it is easy to implement, but at best it provides only a lower limit on the true social willingness to pay for improvements in health and safety, because it neglects the human suffering associated with death, injury, and illness and the amounts that people would be willing to pay to avoid that suffering.

In addition to having a willingness to pay for the productivity gains, individuals in society are presumably willing to pay some amount to see a reduction in the probability that they, or people they care about, will suffer death, injury, or illness. Admittedly, these benefits will be difficult to quantify, but it is nevertheless useful to point out the theoretically correct approach to measuring these benefits and costs. These measurement problems may cause some difficulty in practical applications because it is possible that these individual aspects may be quite large relative to the market output gains. That is, while it may be possible to measure the production aspects of the problem, that measure may considerably underestimate the true magnitude of social willingness to pay for improvements in safety and health.

Let us now turn to a brief description of a few studies that have attempted to obtain measures of these two aspects. First, as far as the production effects go, it is necessary to determine how morbidity and mortality rates will be affected by the project and how this can be translated into increased production or decreased costs. The following examples sketch out how this can be done. Weisbrod (1961) estimated the productivity losses due to premature mortality from polio by obtaining an estimate of the present value of future earnings using data on average earnings and life expectancy and augmenting it with estimates of the value of household services. Then, by using data on deaths caused by polio according to age and sex, he was able to obtain an estimate of the average productivity loss per death from polio. This approach assumes that the value of earnings is the proper measure of productivity, but as we have discussed in the section on the valuation of time above this may not always be the case.

Weisbrod also obtained estimates of output losses due to morbidity by assuming that three months of work time was lost per case because of disability. In addition, he estimated treatment costs from data on the extent of hospital and other medical care given to patients.

Ridker (1967) obtained an estimate of treatment costs for chronic bronchitis using a slightly different approach. He was able to obtain estimates of the total number of patients receiving different types of medical treatment and then by making assumptions about the average treatment costs for the various levels of care, he was able to estimate total cost for each kind of treatment. He also found, by comparing rural and urban morbidity rates, that 20 percent of all cases of chronic bronchitis could be linked to the differences in air quality. He concluded that total treatment costs would fall by 20 percent if air quality in urban areas could be made equal to that in rural areas. Because of the long-term aspects of the disease, of course, these savings would not be achieved for several, perhaps many, years.

As might be imagined, there are very few studies dealing with the non-productivity aspects of this problem. We will discuss two studies that deal with willingness to pay for changes in the probability of death. Thaler and Rosen (1976) examined wage rate differentials across occupations with varying degrees of risk (holding other things equal) and concluded that an increase in the risk of mortality of .001 required a $260 risk premium per year. Jones-Lee (1976) by use of a questionnaire on an admittedly very small sample estimated that on the average, airplane travelers in Britain would be willing to pay six pounds for a reduction of .000002 in the probability of a fatal accident. Comparisons between these two studies are tenuous, but if we can assume that the British trade-off between risk and income is linear, they would pay 3000 pounds for a reduction of .001. The exchange rate fluctuates, but using a £1.6 to $1 exchange rate, we have a range of $260 to $4,800 as an estimate of willingness to pay for a reduction of .001 in the probability of death. This means that for every 1000 people, the total willingness to pay for a .001 reduction in the mortality rate will range from $260,000 to $4,800,000. Since such a reduction would result in one person out of that thousand avoiding a premature death, these figures are estimates of what society is willing to pay to save one life. This is a wide range and we are not prepared to judge which estimate is better. Both studies do, however, approach the question in a conceptually correct manner and we would hope that similar research along these lines will be conducted in the future. In the meantime, these two estimates can be used as rough estimates of the upper and lower bounds.

Value of Recreation

It is often necessary to estimate the willingness to pay for recreational services. For example, one of the benefits of dams or roads may be access to better recreational opportunities. Conversely, the construction and operation of certain facilities may interfere with the enjoyment of recreational opportunities and, as such, this effect should be included as a cost of the project. There are instances where recreational services are sold in a market, but often some other less direct method than using market prices for recreational services must be used to estimate willingness to pay. Fortunately, a good deal of work has been done in developing and refining such methodologies.

Before discussing several of them, it will be worthwhile to dismiss others that have little basis. For instance, the market value of fish is sometimes used as a measure of the willingness to pay for recreational fishing activity, but at best this measure only provides a lower bound estimate. By definition, people do not engage in recreational fishing just for the fish, but rather for the experience of being outdoors and catching (or attempting to catch) the fish. In other instances, the value of a recreational activity has been deemed to be equal to the cost of providing it. That is, if it costs $300,000 to modify a dam so that it will provide a recreation facility, the $300,000 is used as a measure of benefits. This circular reasoning whereby benefits are defined to be equal to costs certainly adds nothing to the decision-making process. Another incorrect method is to measure the value of recreation by summing up the total amount spent by individuals in the process of engaging in recreational activities. This just shows the cost of resources that must be used to engage in the activity, but it does not reveal the social willingness to pay for the recreational activity itself. What we are looking for is the willingness to pay over and above participation costs.

Of the methods that are correct, two derive willingness to pay measures from observation of travel and associated costs. The costs are not used as measures of benefits directly but only as a means to derive one. The first approach that we discuss is the Clawson-Knetsch method, which can best be explained with the aid of a simple example.

Assume that there is a site-specific recreation facility that attracts visitors from three areas. These areas can be towns or cities or concentric semicircular shaped areas around the facility; the only restriction is that all visitors from each area have approximately the same travel costs to the site and that these costs differ among areas. Table 2-1 provides the relevant information about the

Table 2-1
Hypothetical Information for Clawson-Knetsch Method
of Estimating Demand Curve

Area	Population	Visits Made	V/1000	Cost of Visit
1	8000	4400	550	$1
2	3000	1350	450	$3
3	4000	1200	300	$6

areas. The average travel costs per visit (including such items as gas, oil, tolls, and depreciation on cars) for areas 1, 2, and 3 are $1, $3, and $6, respectively. With no admission fee to the site, the number of visits made from each area will be a function of these travel costs and other determinants of recreational visits. Using standard statistical procedures it is possible to obtain an estimate of how visits per capita will be affected by dollar (travel) costs, other things equal. With these contrived figures the relationship is:

$$Visits/1000 = 600 - 50\ C.$$

That is, visits per one thousand population will decrease by 50 for every one dollar increase in associated costs (C). If the populations of the three areas are approximately similar in income distribution and ethnic mix, then it is proper to use this equation (derived from data on all of the areas) to predict how individuals in each will react to changes in costs. (If they are not similar it may be necessary to partition the data so that several equations can be estimated—one each for similar groups in the areas.) This information gives us a basis for deriving a demand curve.

For example, we already know how many visits there will be at a zero price; it is merely the sum of the visits listed in table 2-1. To find how the number of visits will change when there is a $1 admission fee, it is necessary to predict how the individuals in each area will respond. In area 1, the cost per visit will now be $2 ($1 for travel cost and $1 for the admission fee), so using the above equation we can predict that visits per thousand will be 500 from this group. Since the population of this area is 8000, there will be 4000 visits with the $1 fee. Similarly, in area 2 the cost per visit will now be $4 and so visits per thousand will be 400 and total visits will be 1200. In area 3, the cost per visit becomes $7 and visits per thousand will be 250 and total visits will be 1000. The total number of visits with the $1 fee will be the sum of those from the three areas, or 6200. This quantity represents another point on the demand curve. The same procedure can be used for other hypothetical entrance fees and by so doing the complete demand curve as pictured in figure 2-13 can be derived.

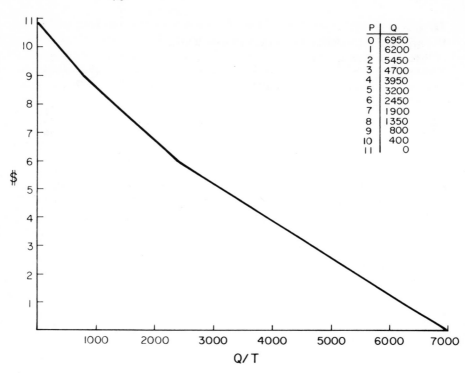

P	Q
0	6950
1	6200
2	5450
3	4700
4	3950
5	3200
6	2450
7	1900
8	1350
9	800
10	400
11	0

Figure 2-13. Demand Curve for Recreation

This demand curve can be used to predict how the number of visits will change with different admission fees. As such it will be a useful planning tool for the park administrator who is concerned with congestion and would like to restrict the number of participants or who must raise revenue and would like to establish an optimal pricing policy. With regard to the last point, a price of $5 would be optimal if the administrator's main objective was to maximize park revenues. From the viewpoint of the benefit-cost analyst, these uses of the curve are of only secondary importance. We are not concerned with revenues received per se, but rather with the value of the services provided as measured by willingness to pay. For example, the total willingness to pay for the services provided when there is a zero admission fee is the complete area under the derived demand curve. This area can be approximated in the following way. There are 6950 visits with no fee and 6200 of them would still be made if the fee were raised to $1. Therefore, the willingness to pay for the facilities must be at least $6200. Since 5450 of those 6200 visits would still be made if the fee were raised by another dollar, then we must add another $5450 to aggregate willingness to pay. If this procedure of raising the fee by one dollar and seeing how many visits are still made is continued until the number of visits falls to zero, it can be seen that total willingness to pay per period for the recreational services is approximately equal to $30,400. (Of course, more sophisticated techniques can be employed to more accurately estimate the total area under a demand curve; for instance, see the illustration of the water development project in chapter 1.) This amount is the annual benefit of constructing a similar project or, alternatively, the annual cost of using the area for some other purpose that precludes its use as a recreation site. (To find the actual total value of this stream of recreational services, it will be necessary to find the *present value* of the future benefits; we consider this aspect of benefit-cost analysis in the next chapter.)

There are some weaknesses with the Clawson-Knetsch method. It can be used to directly estimate the opportunity cost of using an existing recreational area as the site for a proposed project. It is, however, impossible to use it on a site to be developed as a recreational area because the basic data must come from existing visitors. Comparisons with similar projects elsewhere may nevertheless provide useful information in such cases. In addition, the Clawson-Knetsch approach to deriving the demand for recreational services tends to understate true willingness to pay for such services. It focuses only on the financial costs of travel (for instance, expenditures on gas, oil, and tolls) ignoring the fact that the time expended in traveling to a recreational site also represents a cost and, thus, should be taken into account in estimating willingness to pay for recreational services. The relevance of this point for the benefit-cost analyst is that this understatement will lead to an underestimate of consumers' surplus (that is, an underestimate of the benefits potential visitors would receive from a recreational area). There have been attempts in the literature to correct for this problem (Cesario 1976). However, even if it is not corrected, the fact that this method produces an underestimate means that the results can be quite useful as a lower bound measure of willingness to pay.

The method is of little use when travel costs are virtually unmeasurable as in the case of urban parks. Its effectiveness is also lessened when the purpose of the travel is for other things as well (as in the case of most visits to the Grand Canyon) and when the recreational activity (for example, hunting) is not site-specific.

Pearse (1968) has developed a method of estimating recreation benefits that corrects for the problem concerning site-specificity. He estimated the value of mountain hunting by using data on the distance traveled, the costs of arriving at the various hunting sites fully prepared to hunt, and incomes. He first broke his sample into residents and nonresidents and then broke each of these groups into different income classes. He then hypothesized that within each income class, the tastes of the individuals were approximately the same, and that the hunter with the highest cost was just at the margin of deciding not to hunt. He concluded that the difference between what other individuals in each group paid and what the marginal hunter paid was a measure of willingness to pay rather than do without the recreational services. For example, assume that the costs in one of his income groups was as follows:

Hunter 1	$500
Hunter 2	325
Hunter 3	300
Hunter 4	275

According to this method, hunters 2, 3, and 4 would pay $175, $200, and $225 respectively, rather than forego hunting. Therefore, we can conclude that the average consumers' surplus at a zero admission fee for individuals in this income class is $150. Obviously, to place any reliance on these figures the samples would have to be much bigger than that used in this simple example. In any event, by estimating the average consumers' surplus for the various income groups of the residents and nonresidents and then applying these values to the actual number of visitors from each of these categories, an estimate of the total willingness to pay for all users can be obtained. This method has weaknesses, the most important of which is that it can be quite sensitive to the way the income classifications are delineated. Nonetheless, it can provide a useful first approximation to social willingness to pay for the recreational activity.

Willingness to pay for recreational activities can also be obtained by proper use of questionnaires. One problem with this method, of course, is getting people to reveal their true feelings. If people believe that as a result of the questionnaire they may be taxed to pay for the services they use, they will be motivated to give an underestimate; on the other hand, if they feel that they will not be taxed but the results could have an effect on future provision of services, they may overestimate their willingness to pay. It is hard to predict in advance which of these two forces will be stronger. In order to get around these problems it is necessary to properly phrase the questions and to attempt to ask the same thing in different ways in different parts of the questionnaire. A good example of using the questionnaire technique is provided by Hammack and Brown (1974) in their study of the value of waterfowl and wetlands. In one part of their questionnaire, after emphasizing that it is only a hypothetical question, they ask the respondent to estimate the smallest amount he would take to sell his right to hunt waterfowl for a season. Later they ask by how much costs would have to increase before the respondent would stop hunting voluntarily. The answers to both questions provide information on willingness to pay. These estimates were then compared with such things as income, seasons hunted, and success rates. Using standard statistical techniques it was possible to set up an equation to estimate willingness to pay for the entire population from values for the above variables. The questionnaire technique is very exacting and expensive and if it is felt that such a survey is necessary, it would be wise to consult an experienced survey researcher.

As a last resort, the problem of estimating the value of recreation benefits can be approached from a different direction. If it is possible to obtain an estimate of the actual number of recreation days that will be provided by a project, it is sometimes useful to attach hypothetical unit values to the user-days and see how the results of the benefit-cost analysis change as different values are employed. For example, if a project that will eliminate a recreation area passes all benefit-cost tests even if a unit value of $500 for a day of picnicking is used, then there does not appear to be much reason to look into the matter further. The same thing applies if a proposed recreation project has favorable results with a unit value of say $1 for a recreational day. More information may not add much to the decision process. However, if the results of the analysis are quite sensitive to small changes in unit values selected over some reasonable range, then more research is probably necessary. It should be emphasized that this is not a method for estimating benefits, rather it is just a way of looking at the problem of making the proper decision when recreational benefits can be important.

Value of Environmental Externalities

It will be recalled that the basic definition of a benefit is the total willingness to pay for the direct outputs of the project. It is important to keep in mind that the term *direct output* includes everything produced, not just those goods and services for which the project was designed. For example, the direct output of nuclear power plants is electricity, nuclear wastes, heated water from the cooling systems, and so forth. A complete analysis should consider each of these effects, and if some are given relatively little attention it should be because they are thought to be small, not because they are a nonmarketable output. That is, the heated water from the cooling system and the effects it has on the value of goods and services produced is just as important an aspect of a benefit-cost analysis as is the electricity. This point is very important. If it can be appreciated by benefit-cost analysts and decisionmakers alike, it would represent a long step toward improving the framework for decisionmaking. While all of the effects of such things cannot be accurately measured at present, acknowledging their importance will spur research and data collection activities so that our ability to measure such effects will improve, and in the meantime due consideration can be given these problems.

The topic of measuring the costs of environmental damages (or of the benefits of environmental improvement) is very broad and a complete coverage is beyond the scope of this book. The goal of this section will be to establish a framework for looking at the problem and then to discuss very briefly some of the studies that have been done. The reader interested in a more detailed discussion of the ways to measure these effects is referred to an excellent work by Maler and Wyzga (1976).

Perhaps the best way to view this general problem is to use the materials balance approach as developed by Kneese, Ayres, and d'Arge (1970). According to this approach, the economic process is, quite correctly, viewed as just one part of an environment which also includes physical, biological, and chemical processes. The act of production and consumption is really nothing more than taking existing elements and transforming them into items more useful to man. In the process energy is used, heat is given off, and sooner or later the materials are returned to the environment. When the materials from one person's production or consumption are returned to the environment in such a way that the production or consumption of others is affected, we have environmental externalities or pollution.

In order to measure the damage that these undesirable externalities cause, it is useful to break the process into two steps. First, it is necessary to precisely define how the release of the materials will affect the relevant component of the environment. Then it is necessary to see how these changes will affect the economic process. To use the example of a nuclear power plant, we must know first how the release of a specified amount of water heated a certain amount above the ambient temperature of the receiving waters will affect the environment— how will it affect the physical, biological, and chemical processes that make up the ecological system? Then it is necessary to specify how these changes will affect the production and consumption of goods and services from this part of the environment. For example, the heated water may reduce the breeding capacity of a certain stock of fish, and this in turn will reduce the harvest of fish for food as well as the value of a recreational fishing day because the chance of catching suitable fish has diminished. In addition, the heated water may kill flora on the bottom, thus allowing wave action to increase the turbidity of the water. This may also affect the fish stock and, in addition, may have a direct effect on the value of consumption services by diminishing the enjoyment of walks along the beach.

This description should make it clear that before we can obtain accurate estimates of environmental damages it will be necessary to have a much better knowledge of how the environment is affected by changes in the amounts, kinds, locations, and rates of release of various sorts of waste products. This statement is not meant to chastise the scientists who do research in this area; rather it is merely an acknowledgment of the enormous size of the problem. It is equally true that economists' ability to measure the effects of changes in the environment on the value of goods and services produced is far from perfected. But it is hoped that by maintaining a proper view on the subject and by working toward the common goal of finding the answers to the questions thus posed, our ability to obtain these measures and hence our ability to make the proper decisions concerning the use of environmental resources will be constantly improving.

To return to the subject at hand, it is often useful to begin the assessment of the damages of environmental externalities by separating them into financial damages and amenity damages, as suggested by Maler and Wyzga. The financial damages are the productivity losses and increased expenses caused by pollution-related ill health and premature deaths, reduced crop production and forest growth, reduced production from living resources, and the extra costs related to the shortened life or reduced productivity of capital goods such as factories, roads, and so on. Amenity losses are the reductions in the value of goods and services produced directly by the environment. These losses can be measured by the social willingness to pay for the pleasure of fishing, hunting, and viewing wildlife or flowers and, to be complete, to view unsoiled and undamaged buildings, bridges, aesthetic monuments, and other scenery.

An example of estimating financial damage is provided by the study on air pollution corrosion costs by Fink, Buttner, and Boyd (1971) as reported by Maler and Wyzga. They estimated the cost per square foot of painting steel storage tanks and the differences in the maintenance schedule depending upon the air quality conditions of the area in which the tank is located. They found that tanks in relatively clean rural areas had to be painted every twelve years, while those in urban areas needed maintenance every eight years. The difference between the present value of maintenance cost in the two areas is the damage caused by low air quality. They were able to estimate this difference per square foot of surface area and then by multiplying it by the estimated total square feet exposed to air pollution, they obtained an estimate of the total financial damage due to material decay.

As an example of estimating amenity gains from environmental improvements consider the demand curves for recreation in figure 2-13 derived using the travel cost method. Assume that this curve represents demand for the services of a recreational fishery. The area under this curve measures the total willingness to pay for the recreational services. If a pollution control project were undertaken which would increase the size of the fish stock in question, it is likely that the catch rate in the sport fishery would likewise be increased. The increase in people's willingness to pay for recreational fishing that results from the increased catch rate is one of the amenity gains of the project. In order to quantify this effect it is necessary to know the relationship between success rates and fishing activity. Maler and Wyzga report on a study by Stevens (1966) that shows that a 10 percent change in the success rate will change the amount of fishing by around 8 percent. Therefore, if it was determined that the pollution abatement would increase the catch rate by 20 percent, it would be appropriate to increase the number of visits reported in table 2-1 by 16 percent. Then by going through the Clawson-Knetsch procedure again, a new demand curve could be estimated. A comparison of the areas under the old and the new curve will provide an estimate of the increased willingness to pay for recreational fishing.

3

Accounting for Benefits and Costs Over Time

It will normally be the case that all of the benefits and costs from a project do not accrue immediately but over time, perhaps decades. Highways, dams, and ports, for example, all involve construction costs that for the most part occur in the immediate present; however, maintenance costs and most of the benefits from these projects will be experienced for many years into the future. The issue that concerns us in this chapter is how to compare effects occurring immediately with those occurring some time in the future. Since a dollar in the present is worth more than a dollar in the future (because of money's ability to earn interest), we need some method for translating all future dollars into *present value* equivalents. Once all benefits and costs are expressed in present values, they can be readily and justifiably compared with one another.

The format for this chapter is as follows. In the next section we shall illustrate the nature of the problem created by time streams of benefits and costs, and the conventional approach to making present and future effects commensurable. In the following section we shall illustrate the importance of *discounting* (that is, making future effects commensurable with present effects), and consider some alternative notions of how to determine the appropriate discount rate (the actual number used in converting future values into present values). In the next-to-the-last section we shall discuss the conventional benefit-cost criteria for accepting or rejecting projects. The concluding section presents some summary recommendations in connection with accounting for benefits and costs over time.

The Problem and its Resolution: An Illustration

The main problems posed by projects that yield time streams of benefits and costs are easily illustrated within the context of the following example. Suppose that a governmental agency is considering whether to improve the insulation in an aging government office building that is to be replaced by a new building at the end of two years. The cost of better insulation is $5,000, whereas the anticipated savings in heating and cooling costs is $2,800 for each of the two remaining years in the building's life. Should the agency proceed with this project?

Superficially, it might appear that this particular project is worthwhile since a $5,000 outlay today saves $5,600 in heating and cooling costs over the next two years. However, such reasoning is incorrect because it overlooks the time

77

value of money. The question the analyst should seek to answer in this case is the following: "Is the present value of the anticipated savings in heating and cooling costs greater or less than $5,000, the cost of insulating the building?" An alternative, but equivalent, way of framing this question is: "Would the agency earn more or less than the $2,800 per year offered by the insulation project by placing the initial $5,000 into an alternative investment (for example, in stocks or bonds)?" The first way of framing this question focuses upon the *discounting* of future dollars into present values, whereas the second approach concentrates on the translation of present dollars (the $5,000 initial outlay) into a time stream of future dollars (that is, it focuses on *compounding*).

In principle these approaches to making present and future dollars commensurable are equivalent. However, in practice there are advantages (discussed below) to expressing all dollar estimates in terms of present values. Consequently, in this chapter we are ultimately interested in carefully explaining and illustrating the present-value method. However, the compounding concept (the obverse of discounting) is more widely used and, therefore, more easily understood than the discounting (present value) concept, so there is some heuristic advantage in expositing the compounding method first and then turning to a discussion of discounting. This is the approach we follow.

Compounding

As noted above, one alternative confronting the agency is to spend $5,000 on insulating the building and thereby save an anticipated $2,800 per year for two years. In addition, suppose that the agency has the opportunity to invest the $5,000 in a financial asset (a stock or a bond) offering an annual rate of return (net of any commissions or other costs) equal to 10 percent. To determine which of these alternatives is preferable, we can translate the initial $5,000 into a two-year time stream with the aid of the well-known compounding formula:

$$FV_n = PV(1 + r)^n,$$

where PV is the amount invested today (the present value), r is the annual rate of return (10 percent in the above example), n is the number of years that PV will be earning the compound rate of return, and FV_n (the future value) equals the initial investment plus all the compound interest earnings after n years. If the rate of return is expected to vary over time, the compounding formula would be rewritten as:

$$FV_n = PV[(1 + r_1)(1 + r_2)(1 + r_3) \ldots (1 + r_{n-1})(1 + r_n)].$$

If the agency decides not to insulate the building, the compounding formula suggests that at the end of the first year the agency could have $5,500—the initial $5,000 plus $500 in interest earnings ($5,500 = $5,000 × 1.10). Assuming for simplicity that the agency's energy costs are paid only once a year (at year's end), the agency would have $2,700 remaining after payment of the $2,800 energy bill. If the $2,700 is reinvested at 10 percent, the agency will have at the end of the second year $2,970 ($2,700 × 1.10), or $170 remaining after payment of the $2,800 energy bill. In effect, if the insulation strategy is pursued, the agency gets $2,800 each year in return for the original $5,000 investment (an implicit rate of return of about 8 percent), whereas the financial investment provides revenues of $2,800 the first year and $2,970 the second. Clearly, the agency would be foolish to forego the opportunity to earn a 10 percent rate of return in order to earn an implicit 8 percent of return.

Alternatively, suppose the return available on the financial asset was 5 percent, rather than 10 percent. If the insulation is not installed, the agency could have $5,250 ($5,000 × 1.05) at the end of the first year, or $2,450 after payment of the $2,800 heating and cooling costs that would have otherwise been saved. By the end of the second year, there would only be $2,573 ($2,450 × 1.05) available from the original $5,000, implying that an additional $227 would have to be raised to pay the $2,800 energy bill. In this instance, the agency would be well advised to invest the original $5,000 to improve the building's insulation (thereby earning an 8 percent rate of return) rather than purchasing a financial asset yielding 5 percent annually.

Discounting

In the preceding discussion we evaluated the alternative investment strategies by comparing the annual benefits of the two equal-cost investments. An alternative approach to this evaluation is to convert the future effects into present values.

The *present value* (*PV*) of some future sum (*FV*) is the amount of money that would just make the recipient indifferent between receiving *PV* now and receiving *FV* at some specified time in the future. The present value calculation is relatively straightforward; in fact, it is just a variation on the conventional compound-sum calculation discussed above. The compounding formula is easily converted to a present value formula by simply dividing both sides of the equation by $(1 + r)^n$:

$$PV = FV_n/(1 + r)^n$$

where r is now referred to as a *discount rate*.

To illustrate the use of the present value concept, let us return to the insulation example. The present value of the savings in energy costs is ($2,800/1.10 + $2,800/1.10^2) or $4,860 when the opportunity cost of the agency's funds is 10 percent. When this present value of the benefit stream is compared with the $5,000 cost, it is obvious that it is not a wise decision to undertake the project.

By comparison, if the agency confronts a 5 percent opportunity cost for its funds, the present value of the annual $2,800 energy savings is ($2,800/1.05 + $2,800/1.05^2) or $5,206. That is, for a $5,000 outlay today, the agency can obtain benefits worth $5,206 in present dollars.

In this simple example it is just as easy to make the benefit flows from the alternative strategies commensurable on an annual basis as it is to convert the flows into present values, and both approaches lead us to identical conclusions (that is, when the opportunity cost of the agency's funds is 10 percent, the insulation project is not worthwhile; but when the opportunity cost is only 5 percent, the project should be undertaken). However, it is frequently more convenient (and certainly more conventional in benefit-cost studies) to express all dollar estimates in terms of present values. For instance, consider two alternative projects, A and B, either of which would cost $5,000 today and yield benefits over a four-year period. Suppose project A produces a time stream of annual benefits (received at the end of the year) equal to

$$\$3,000 \qquad \$1,000 \qquad \$8,000 \qquad \$2,000$$

whereas project B yields annual benefits of

$$\$4,000 \qquad \$\ 500 \qquad \$6,000 \qquad \$2,400.$$

Which of these two projects is preferable? From a mere comparison of the annual benefits, it is impossible to determine the answer. Project B is preferable in the first and fourth years, but project A is clearly better in the second and third years. However, it is a straightforward task to convert these time streams into commensurable present values, once we have selected a discount rate. Assuming that the discount rate appropriate to this example is 5 percent, it follows that the present value of the benefits from projects A and B are:

Project A

$$\$12,320 = \$3,000/1.05 + \$1,000/1.05^2 + \$8,000/1.05^3 + \$2,000/1.05^4$$

Project B

$$\$11,420 = \$4,000/1.05 + \$500/1.05^2 + \$6,000/1.05^3 + \$2,400/1.05^4.$$

What these calculations mean is that if $12,320 were put in a bank today at 5 percent interest it would be possible to withdraw $3,000, $1,000, $8,000, and $2,000 in the first, second, third and fourth year respectively before the account would be depleted. Similarly $11,420 would yield $4,000, $500, $6,000 and $2,400. It is now possible to make a meaningful comparison between the two projects. Project A is superior to project B because the present value of the stream of benefits is higher.

In general terms then, once the future benefits have been transformed into commensurable present values $(B_n/(1 + r)^n)$, they can be simply added together to obtain a measure of the total present value of all benefits (B_{PV}):

$$B_{PV} = B_0 + \frac{B_1}{(1 + r)} + \frac{B_2}{(1 + r)^2} + \ldots + \frac{B_N}{(1 + r)^N}$$

$$= \sum_{n=0}^{N} \frac{B_n}{(1 + r)^n}$$

where B_n denotes the benefits expected during the nth year. Likewise, the discounted present value of all costs (C_{PV}) can be obtained through an analogous procedure:

$$C_{PV} = C_0 + \frac{C_1}{(1 + r)} + \frac{C_2}{(1 + r)^2} + \ldots + \frac{C_N}{(1 + r)^N}$$

$$= \sum_{n=0}^{N} \frac{C_n}{(1 + r)^n}$$

where C_n measures the anticipated costs for the nth year. Although we have not explicitly discussed it, the above equations also hold if any of the Bs or Cs are negative.

Calculating Present Values

The actual calculation of present values can be greatly simplified through the use of present value tables such as tables A-1 and A-2 (see the appendix). (Of course, even greater computational simplicity is offered by electronic calculators programmed to calculate present values.) To briefly illustrate the use of such tables, we refer first to the example of the two projects (A and B) presented in the preceding section.

The calculation of the present value of, say, project A's benefits involved some rather tedious arithmetic, namely, solving for values of $1/1.05$, $1/1.05^2$, $1/1.05^3$, and $1/1.05^4$. This routine exercise can be avoided entirely by merely referring to a present value table which provides solutions to $1/(1 + r)^n$ for a variety of discount rates and time periods. The expression $1/(1 + r)^n$ is sometimes referred to as the *present value factor*. For example, the entry in table A–1 that corresponds to year 1 and 5 percent is $1/1.05 = .952$, whereas, the entry corresponding to year 2 and 5 percent is $1/1.05^2 = .907$, and so on. Thus, the arithmetic involved in the calculation of the present value of project A's benefits can be reduced to a relatively straightforward:

$$Present\ Value = (\$3,000 \times .952) + (\$1,000 \times .907)$$
$$+ (\$8,000 \times .864) + (\$2,000 \times .823)$$
$$= \$12,320.$$

If the annual flow of either benefits or costs and the discount rate is expected to be constant from year to year, the computation of present values can be simplified even more. Consider, for example, the following four-year time stream of benefits:

$$\$4,000 \qquad \$4,000 \qquad \$4,000 \qquad \$4,000$$

The present value (*PV*) of this benefit flow is:

$$PV = \$4,000/(1 + r) + \$4,000/(1 + r)^2 + \$4,000/(1 + r)^3 + \$4,000/(1 + r)^4$$

which can be rewritten as:

$$PV = \$4,000[1/(1 + r) + 1/(1 + r)^2 + 1/(1 + r)^3 + 1/(1 + r)^4]$$
$$= \$4,000 \sum_{n=1}^{4} 1/(1 + r)^n.$$

Once a value for the discount rate is selected we need only to refer to table A–2, which reveals the present worth of an annuity of \$1 for alternative time periods and discount rates, to find a value for $\sum_{n=1}^{4} 1/(1 + r)^n$. For instance, if the discount rate is 5 percent, the value of this present worth factor is 3.546 (see the entry in table A–2 corresponding to 4 years and 5 percent). Consequently, the present value of this time stream of benefits is simply $\$14,184 = \$4,000 \times 3.546$.

The Discount Rate

An important issue in connection with the discounting of future benefits and costs is the selection of the discount rate; that is, what specific discount rate should be used in translating future benefits and costs into present values? This question is important because the size of the discount rate used can be critical.

Consider a project that involves initial construction costs of $10 million and provides an annual net benefit flow of $800,000 a year for thirty years. Does the present value of these net benefits exceed the $10 million cost? That is, according to strict efficiency criteria, should the project be undertaken? The answer depends on the specific discount rate used. For instance, the present values of this time stream of benefits at discount rates of 3, 7, and 10 percent are:

Discount Rate	Present Value
3%	$15,680,000
7%	$ 9,927,200
10%	$ 7,451,600.

If a 3 percent rate of discount is used, this hypothetical project appears economically efficient since discounted benefits exceed initial costs by $5.68 million. However, with a 7 percent discount rate the project appears marginally inefficient because discounted costs slightly exceed the present value of benefits. Finally, a 10 percent discount rate reveals a project that should clearly be rejected on economic efficiency grounds (since costs exceed benefits by about $2.55 million in present value terms).

An additional illustration of the importance of the discount rate is provided by table 3-1. This table reveals the present value of $1,000 discounted over selected time periods at various discount rates. As indicated, when the discount rate is zero, the present value and future values are identical. A discount rate of zero implies an indifference between equal amounts in the present and the future: $1,000 today is the same as $1,000 thirty years from now. However, as the discount rate is increased, future effects quickly begin to lose their relative importance. For instance, $1,000 to be received thirty years hence is worth only about $2 today when discounted at 15 percent!

Table 3-1
Present Value of $1,000 for Selected Time Periods and Discount Rates

Number of Years Until $1,000 Benefit Received	Discount Rate				
	0%	3%	7%	10%	15%
1	$1,000	$971	$935	$909	$870
5	1,000	863	713	621	497
10	1,000	744	508	386	247
20	1,000	554	258	149	61
30	1,000	412	131	57	2

This tendency for discounting—especially at the higher rates—to quickly diminish the present value of effects in the relatively distant future carries an interesting implication for benefit-cost analysis. In particular, one of the apparently vexing problems confronting the benefit-cost analyst is how to estimate, with any degree of confidence, benefits or costs occurring ten, twenty, thirty or even more years into the future. Frequently, the assignment of values to effects expected to take place this many years in the future involves little more than educated guesswork at best. It is simply not possible—given the present stage of development in the social sciences in general and in benefit-cost analysis in particular—to accurately predict over the long run such things as population shifts, energy crises, taste changes, or technical innovations. Such things are sometimes difficult to accurately predict even over a one or two year period. Fortunately, however, discounting ameliorates this problem.

To illustrate, consider a project that could yield benefits for thirty years, although there is considerable uncertainty regarding the magnitude of the benefits in the later years. Suppose that benefits in the thirtieth year could be as high as $20 million or as low as $1 million. What value should be used in the present-value calculation? The answer is that it may not matter very much whether $1 million or $20 million (or some amount in between these two) is used. If the discount rate employed is relatively high there simply may not be a significant difference between the present values of $1 million and $20 million. For instance, discounting at 10 percent yields present values of $57,000 (for $1 million) and $1,140,000 (for $20 million), that is, the $19 million difference in the future is reduced to around a $1 million difference in present value terms, and such a difference may not affect the outcome of the benefit-cost study. (The issue of uncertainty is treated in greater detail in chapter 4.)

It is quite clear from table 3-1 that increasing the discount rate diminishes the present value of any future effect, and for most projects this means that higher discount rates will yield lower benefit-cost ratios or lower *net* present values (that is, discounted benefits minus discounted costs). For example projects such as dams and highways most commonly incur most of their costs relatively early while the benefits are received over longer periods of time. With such a pattern for benefit and cost flows, higher discount rates do produce lower net present values. However, in the special case where the pattern is reversed and costs exceed benefits in later years (for instance, as they might with rising concentrations of radioactive wastes from nuclear power plants), increases in the discount rate may yield higher net present values because the negative effects of the later years receive less weight.

The size of the discount rate can also be critical for comparing two or more projects. This can be seen by examining figure 3-1. It reveals the effect that changes in the discount rate have on the net present value (present value of benefits minus present value of costs) of two hypothetical projects, C and D. Each project is assumed to cost $5 million in present value terms, and each is expected to yield benefits over a ten year period. It is supposed that project C will provide annual benefits of $1.5 million for each of the ten years, whereas project D will yield $.5 million annually the first 5 years, and $3.5 million annually the last 5 years. With discount rates between zero and 15 percent, project D is preferable to project C, but with discount rates in excess of 15 percent project C becomes the more desirable. If these projects are mutually exclusive, or if a budget constraint prevents the agency from undertaking both projects, the selection of the discount rate will determine which project will be undertaken.

Selection of a Discount Rate

While we have shown the importance of the discount rate in benefit-cost analysis, we have yet to discuss the alternative approaches to determining the appropriate discount rate. In some instances, the selection of a discount rate poses no problem for the benefit-cost analyst, because government agencies specify what discount rate is to be used in benefit-cost studies, leaving the analyst performing a study with no flexibility. This is not to say, of course, that such agencies dictate the appropriate discount rate; it is merely to say that in such circumstances the analyst may have little or no discretion over which rate of discount to use.

The Opportunity Cost of Capital. When the analyst does have some discretion in the selection of a discount rate, one conventional practice (and the one we recommend) is to use a measure of the opportunity cost of capital in the private sector as the discount rate for public sector activities. The rationale for this approach is easily illustrated with the aid of an example.

Suppose that an agency is contemplating undertaking a project that would involve an immediate cost of $1 million but provide net annual benefits of (approximately) $163,000 for ten years, yielding an implicit 10 percent rate of return on the $1 million investment. To undertake this project, funds will have to be transferred from the private sector of the economy. Assume that this is accomplished by raising the tax level in the corporate sector. Suppose that as a result of the additional $1 million in taxes, the corporate sector must forego $1 million of private investment in new plant and equipment that would have yielded net annual benefits to society equal to (approximately) $177,000 over a ten year period (an implicit social rate of return of 12 percent). Obviously, society would be foolish (from a strict efficiency viewpoint) to exchange private sector projects offering a 12 percent rate of return for the public sector projects providing a 10 percent return. The conventional way to assure that such an undesirable transfer of resources from the private to the public sector does not take place is to use the social rate of return to private use of the funds

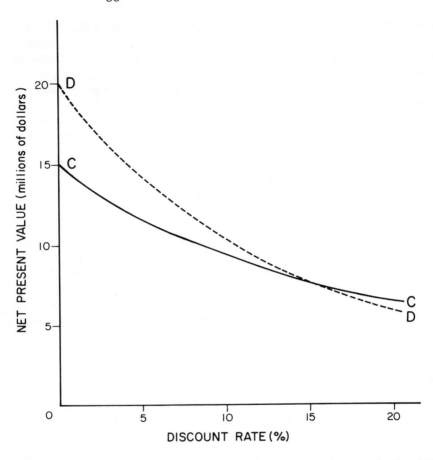

Figure 3-1. The Effect of Discount Rate Changes on the Magnitude of Net Present Value

or resources (that is, the opportunity cost of capital in the private sector) as the discount rate in benefit-cost studies of proposed public sector activities. For example, discounting the $163,000 annual benefit flow from the agency's proposed project in the above example at 12 percent yields $921,000 as the present value of that benefit flow. Since the project would cost $1 million, benefit-cost (efficiency) criteria would therefore indicate that the project should not be undertaken.

If, in this example, the corporate sector projects had been providing a 10 percent return (rather than 12 percent), society would be indifferent (on efficiency grounds) between leaving the resources in the private sector and transferring them to public sector uses. And in fact, if a 10 percent discount rate is used in evaluating the agency's proposal, the present value of the net benefit flow would just equal the $1 million cost of the project, indicating no efficiency advantage from undertaking the project.

Finally, suppose that the average opportunity cost of corporate funds is 8 percent. Discounting the benefit flow from the public sector project at 8 percent produces a present value of benefits equal to (approximately) $1,090,000. In this instance, replacing private sector activities with the public sector project enhances society's welfare (in an efficiency sense).

The conclusion that can be drawn from these illustrations is the following. Using the rate of return on the funds or productive resources, were they to remain in their alternative uses (presumably in the private sector), as the discount rate in evaluating public sector activities assures that, on efficiency grounds, only those public sector activities offering a rate of return in excess of that available in the private sector will be undertaken. Alternatively, this conclusion can be summarized notationally as follows (where r_g is the estimated percent rate of return on a proposed public sector activity, r_p is the percent rate of return available in the private sector, B_{pv} is the present value of the benefits from the proposed project, and C_{pv} is the present value of costs):

(a) If $r_g > r_p$, then $B_{pv} > C_{pv}$;
(b) if $r_g = r_p$, then $B_{pv} = C_{pv}$; and
(c) if $r_g < r_p$, then $B_{pv} < C_{pv}$;

as long as r_p is used as the discount rate.

It will normally be the case that the relevant measure of the rate of return to resources in the private sector will be a weighted average of several rates of return, since tax revenues come from different sectors of the economy. To illustrate the logic underlying the computation of such an average opportunity cost, suppose that a proposed $1 million government project would be financed with $500,000 from the corporate sector and $500,000 from individuals. Suppose further that the average rate of return in the corporate sector is 15 percent before taxes; that corporate earnings are taxed at a marginal rate of 50 percent; that in response to the additional $500,000 tax on individuals, consumers reduce consumption by $400,000 and savings by $100,000 (the marginal propensity to consume is 0.8); that the average return to individual savings is 6 percent before taxes and 5 percent after taxes; that individual savings are invested by financial intermediaries in the corporate sector; and, finally, that the economy is fully employed so that this balanced-budget increase in government activity has no effect on the economy other than those mentioned above.

Which rate of return, or combination of rates, represents the opportunity cost of removing resources from the private sector? The answer is that the appropriate measure of opportunity cost is a weighted average of the individual rates of return, where the weights for each sector are determined by the amount of the resources being taken from that sector relative to the total amount of resources being expended. Thus, in the present example, the weights are 0.5 for the corporate rate of return (r_c), 0.1 for the social return on savings (r_s), and 0.4 for the implicit rate of return to consumption (r_i). That is, the overall opportunity cost (r_p) of extracting resources from private use in the proportions indicated is computed (in this example) as:

$$r_p = .5r_c + .4r_i + .1r_s.$$

The remaining issue now is what are the appropriate values for r_c, r_i, and r_s? The social rate of return to corporate investment is the before-tax return (15 percent by assumption) rather than the after-tax return (7.5 percent in this example). The payment of taxes transfers some corporate earnings to the public sector, but (generally) this involves only a redistribution of the rewards for producing socially desirable goods and services. Consequently, the 15 percent before-tax rate of return measures the social gain from corporate investments, even though only one-half of that gain remains in the hands of the corporations and their stockholders.

The $100,000 reduction in personal savings actually implies (in the present example) an additional $100,000 reduction in corporate investment: the reduced savings leads the financial intermediaries to cut back their loans to the corporate sector by $100,000 which, in turn, occasions a similar decrease in corporate investment spending. Thus, the social cost of the reduced savings is 15 percent (the before-tax return to corporate investment), not the 6 percent before-tax financial return to private savings.

Finally, the implicit social return to private consumption expenditures is measured by the 5 percent after-tax return to savings. It may seem puzzling to measure the return to consumption in this fashion. However, the underlying logic is quite compelling. Since there is no explicit rate of return earned on consumption expenditures, it must be estimated indirectly. The rationale for using the return to savings as a proxy for the implicit return to consumption expenditures is that individuals will equate, on the margin, the implicit return available from consumption to that available from savings. If individuals can earn 5 percent after taxes on their savings, they will allocate their incomes between consumption and savings so that the implicit return to the last consumption expenditure just equals 5 percent. If the implicit rate of return to marginal consumption was less than 5 percent, the individual would consume less and save more until the marginal rates of return were equalized. Alternatively, if the implicit return to consumption was greater than 5 percent, the individual would consume more and save less, again until the marginal rates of return were equalized. Of course, some individuals may consume all of their income, implying that, for them, the marginal return to consumption expenditures exceeds the marginal return to savings at a zero level of savings. For such individuals, we simply cannot infer the implicit rate of return to consumption. A conservative approach to resolving this problem is to still use the rate of return to private savings, which in fact does serve as an accurate lower bound estimate of the return to consumption expenditures.

Applying the information that r_c = .15, r_i = .05, and r_s = .15, we can compute the weighted average rate of return to private expenditures (in this example) as 11 percent (.5(.15) + .4(.05) + .1(.15)). Of course, in the general case, the weighted average rate of return (r_p) is calculated as:

$$r_p = w_1 r_1 + w_2 r_2 + \ldots + w_j r_j + \ldots + w_J r_J$$

where w_j is the weight for the jth sector (that is, the proportion of the total funds coming from the jth sector) and r_j is the social rate of return to expenditures in the jth sector.

Haveman (1969) found that the appropriate weighted average for 1966 was about 7.3 percent. However, this figure may no longer accurately reflect the present opportunity cost of private sector expenditures. A replication of Haveman's study with current data could very well yield a substantially different measure of the opportunity cost of private sector expenditures because of changes in private sector rates of return.

The preceding analysis also applies to situations involving debt, rather than tax, financing of projects. In principle, the appropriate discount rate remains the rate of return foregone in the private sector as a result of transferring resources to public sector activities. In order to determine this rate, it is necessary to find out what types of investment will be precluded and what rates of return would be earned. Although funds may be raised by borrowing at 5 percent, for example, this may preclude investment in the corporate sector at 15 percent (before taxes), and the latter rate is the actual opportunity cost.

A slightly different approach may be used for state or local projects with narrowly defined accounting stances. In this case the rate at which the governmental unit can borrow can be used as a discount rate. The rationale for this suggestion is essentially a pragmatic one—state or local officials are normally interested in undertaking only those projects that confer net benefits upon their constituents. They cannot be expected to pursue policies that would enhance efficiency nationwide unless those same policies enhance efficiency locally. If a locality, for example, can borrow unlimited amounts at 5 percent, it can increase local welfare by undertaking all projects yielding rates of return in excess of 5 percent; that is, it should discount all benefits and costs at 5 percent. This approach may, of course, mean that investment projects elsewhere that earn a higher rate may be precluded. For more on the pros and cons of narrow accounting stances refer to the discussion in chapter 2.

Social Discount Rate. There is a view that holds that the private (weighted average) opportunity cost of capital is inappropriate for discounting the future effects of public sector projects. Advocates of this position maintain, for example, that individuals are "myopic" in their consumption and savings decisions. Supposedly, people systematically underestimate the value of future consumption and consequently save less and consume more than is socially optimal. In addition, it has been argued that current generations do not adequately take into account the welfare of future generations, again, saving less and consuming more than is socially desirable. Finally, it has been pointed out that investment, especially in underdeveloped economies, may entail substantial external benefits (in terms of making other investments profitable), implying that the private marketplace will generate suboptimal levels of saving and investment.

All of these reasons have been put forth as justification for using a social discount rate that is less than the private opportunity cost of capital. Presumably this social discount rate would have to be given to the analyst by, say, a legislature since there is no conventional method for estimating it. Supposedly, lowering the discount rate for public sector projects below the private opportunity cost of capital will result in more projects satisfying the benefit-cost criteria and, consequently, in higher levels of investment. Unfortunately, the undertaking of additional public sector investment may lead to some crowding out of private sector investment, thereby having little, if any, effect on the aggregate level of investment. In fact, this crowding-out phenomenon would lower an economy's productive potential if the displaced private investment offered a higher return than the incremental public sector investment.

If the above argument is accepted, the proper policy implication is to stimulate aggregate investment (private and public) until the rate of return being earned in both sectors is equal to the social rate of return. This will guarantee that there is a proper intertemporal use of resources. But if the social rate of return is only used in determining public investment, it will lead to allocational inefficiency in the current use of resources. (For a more detailed discussion of a social rate of discount and the pros and cons of its use in benefit-cost analysis, the reader is referred to the works of Feldstein, Sen, and Marglin.)

Sensitivity Analysis

While there is some controversy over what constitutes the appropriate procedure for arriving at a discount rate, in many instances this controversy need not concern the benefit-cost analyst. In particular, it will frequently be the case that the exact value selected for the discount rate simply will not affect, in any significant way, the outcome of the benefit-cost study. Some projects will offer such a high (or low) rate of return that they would appear desirable (or undesirable) according to benefit-cost criteria regardless of the discount rate employed (assuming it to be a reasonable rate, say, between 5 and 15 percent). However, the exact value of the discount rate may be critical in other situations, such as those involving mutually exclusive projects, budget-constrained agencies, or projects that appear efficient for some discount rates but inefficient for others.

The conventional method for identifying those situations in which the exact value of the discount rate is crucial is to perform a sensitivity analysis, that is, to calculate the present value of benefits and costs for at least two alternative discount rates. Normally, the analyst should select a relatively low discount rate (for example, 5 percent) and a relatively high rate (say, 15 percent) in order to test the sensitivity of the benefit-cost estimates to changes in the discount rate. If the analysis reveals that the benefit-cost measures are relatively insensitive to changes in the discount rate, the matter essentially ends there; however, if the study's findings are sensitive to the particular discount rate selected, the analyst must make that fact known to policymakers so that they might make their own judgments regarding the appropriate magnitude for the discount rate. We will return to this issue in chapter 5, which discusses the presentation of the benefit-cost results.

Inflation and the Discount Rate

During periods of inflation, the analyst must take care to avoid having purely inflationary effects influence the outcome of the benefit-cost study. To illustrate how a general price inflation can affect a benefit-cost analysis and how spurious influences can be eliminated, we consider the following simple example.

Suppose a proposed project offers an annual net benefit stream (assuming no inflation) of $1 million over three years for an immediate outlay of $2.49 million—an implicit rate of return of 10 percent. Supposing further that the private opportunity cost of capital (also assuming no anticipated inflation) is 8 percent, the proposed project would appear desirable according to benefit-cost criteria, since discounting the future benefits at 8 percent yields a present value of benefits equal to $2.58 million.

Suppose, however, that an annual 5 percent general price inflation is anticipated for the foreseeable future. If this expected inflation is incorporated into the estimated future net benefits, the benefit stream (rather than being $1 million annually) would be $1.05 million, $1.10 million, and $1.16 million, respectively, for each of the three years. Obviously, discounting this benefit stream at 8 percent would yield an even higher present value of benefits, suggesting apparently that the anticipated inflation enhances the efficiency value of the project. However, this latter suggestion should be rejected on the grounds that the 8 percent discount rate (assumed appropriate for a noninflationary period) is no longer appropriate. If capital markets have fully adjusted to the anticipated 5 percent inflation, we would expect the private opportunity cost of capital to rise in tandem with the rate of inflation. In the absence of inflation, a $1 million, one-year investment in the private sector would, on average, return $1.08 million after one year (an 8 percent return). With a 5 percent inflation expected, the payoff at the end of the one year would presumably be $1.134 million (1.08 million × 1.05), for an implicit rate of return of 13.4 percent. Thus, a 5 percent fully anticipated inflation can be expected, other things equal, to increase the private opportunity cost of capital from 8 percent to 13.4 percent.

Using a discount rate of 13.4 percent to obtain the present value of the three-year time stream of inflated benefits ($1.05 million, $1.10 million, and $1.16 million) yields exactly $2.58 million, precisely the same estimate obtained for the noninflationary situation.

The conclusion to be drawn from this analysis, therefore, is that inflation can be appropriately handled by either of two methods: (1) estimate all future benefits and costs in constant prices (that is, simply assume no inflation) and use, as the discount rate, an estimate of the private opportunity cost of capital in the absence of anticipated inflation, or (2) estimate all future effects in current (that is, inflated) prices and use as the discount rate an estimate of the private opportunity cost of capital in the presence of the anticipated rate of inflation.

Unfortunately, regardless of the approach taken, the analyst encounters some difficulties that are not easily resolved. The first approach requires that the analyst make some judgment about the private opportunity cost of capital in the absence of inflation. When inflation is anticipated, the perceived (or nominal) return to private investment (or consumption) contains an inflation premium that may be very difficult to estimate. If the current rate of inflation is used as an estimate of the inflation premium, it will occasionally be the case that the implied real return to private expenditures is negative! On the other hand, if the second approach is pursued, the analyst is confronted with the problem of predicting the rate of inflation for perhaps many years into the future.

In practice, it is probably the case that most analysts estimate future benefits and costs in constant prices, that is, they essentially ignore inflation. As an approximation to the private opportunity cost of capital in an inflation-free situation, it appears to be common practice to arbitrarily select some "plausible" rate of return (say, 10 percent) for discounting the benefits and costs of public sector projects. (See the above discussion on sensitivity analysis.)

Alternative Benefit-Cost Criteria

There are three criteria for accepting or rejecting projects. These alternative criteria, and their associated decision rules (which account for efficiency effects only) are:

Criteria	Decision Rule
1. Benefit-cost ratio, B/C (the ratio of the present value of benefits and costs).	1. Accept if $B/C > 1$; reject if $B/C < 1$.
2. Net present value, $B - C$ (the difference between the present value of benefits and the present value of costs).	2. Accept if $B - C > 0$; reject if $B - C < 0$.
3. Internal rate of return (that rate of return—or discount rate—that just equates discounted benefits to discounted costs).	3. Accept if the internal rate of return exceeds the private opportunity cost of capital; otherwise reject.

It will be recalled from chapter 1 that the basis for benefit-cost analysis is the Hicks-Kaldor criteria; that is, a project is considered to be economically efficient if it results in an increase in the value of goods and services produced. It is easy to see that all three of these benefit-cost criteria are alternative ways of determining if the Hicks-Kaldor criteria is met. Since benefits of a project are the increase in the value of output and costs are the value of the opportunities foregone, if $B/C > 1$ or $B - C > 0$, then it is obvious that there has been a net increase in the value of production. The same conclusion holds if the internal rate of return is greater than the private opportunity cost of capital.

As an illustration of these criteria, consider again the $2.49 million project providing benefits of $1 million annually for three years. Assuming an 8 percent discount rate (equal to the private opportunity cost of capital), we obtain the following:

$$\frac{B}{C} = \frac{\$1 \text{ million}/1.08 + \$1 \text{ million}/1.08^2 + \$1 \text{ million}/1.08^3}{\$2.49 \text{ million}}$$

$$= \frac{\$2.58 \text{ million}}{\$2.49 \text{ million}} = 1.036$$

$$B - C = \$2.58 \text{ million} - \$2.49 \text{ million}$$
$$= \$90,000$$

Internal rate of return:
$1 million$/(1 + x) + \$1$ million$/(1 + x)^2 + \$1$ million$/(1 + x)^3 = 2.49$ million, where $x =$ the internal rate of return; in this case $x = .10$ or 10 percent.

It should be obvious that the internal rate of return is the most difficult to use since it involves the solution of a difficult algebraic equation. There are, however, many computer programs that can solve these equations using an interative numerical process. In any event, all three decision criteria indicate that, on efficiency grounds, the project should be undertaken.

If only one project is under consideration, or if there is no binding budget constraint (so that all acceptable projects can be undertaken), and all of the projects under consideration are independent of one another (ruling out mutually exclusive projects), then the analyst can use either benefit-cost ratios or net present values. Under the assumed circumstances, the two criteria will always agree as to the desirability of a project.

Usually, although not always, the internal rate of return criteria will yield results identical to the other two criteria. Unfortunately, it is possible for a time stream of benefits and costs to imply more than one internal rate of return, that is, for the equation above to have more than one solution. For instance, consider a project involving an initial cost of $1 million, a net benefit of $2.2 million at the end of the first year, and a net second-year cost of $1.2 million. This time stream yields internal rates of return of 0 and 20 percent (obtained by solving the equation, $-\$1$ million $+ \$2.2$ million$/(1 + r) - \$1.2$ million$/(1 + r)^2 = 0$, for r). Suppose the private opportunity cost of capital to be 10 percent. Should this project be undertaken or not? Is it a very good investment yielding an implicit return of 20 percent, or is it a very poor one offering no positive rate of return whatsoever?

The simplest way to resolve this problem is to discount all future effects back to the present, using the private opportunity cost of capital as the discount rate. This approach yields $1,999,800 as the present value of the benefits and $1,991,200 as the present value of the costs, suggesting that at this discount rate the project would be marginally beneficial. In this example however any discount rate between 0 and 20 percent would suggest that the project should be undertaken on efficiency grounds.

One might infer from this example that the two internal rates of return merely provide the analyst with information about the maximum and minimum discount rates (0 and 20 percent) that would yield positive (or zero) discounted net benefits. Under certain circumstances such an inference would be correct, but under other circumstances it would be seriously misleading. To illustrate, let us simply alter the preceding example slightly, so that the time stream is $1 million, $-\$2.2$ million, and $+\$1.2$ million (rather than $-\$1$ million, $+\$2.2$ million, and $-\$1.2$ million). This flow also implies internal rates of return of 0 and 20 percent. However, discounting these effects back to the present with rates between 0 and 20 percent yields discounted costs in excess of discounted benefits! Only if this time stream is discounted with rates less than zero or greater than 20 percent would the project appear desirable on efficiency grounds.

From the above discussion, we can conclude that while it may prove pedagogically useful to calculate and refer to internal (or implicit) rates of return, it will normally be advisable for the benefit-cost analyst to use net present values, or benefit-cost ratios, since they are easier to calculate and much less ambiguous. To summarize the results so far, any project which passes either of these criteria (if it passes one it must pass the other) should be undertaken on strict efficiency grounds.

It is often the case, however, that all such projects cannot be used by the public sector, either because some may be mutually exclusive (for instance, building a dam at a particular site may preclude building another at a nearby location) or because of budget constraints on an agency's behavior. In these cases the problem is to select the superior projects from the acceptable ones. In this case the net present value and benefit-cost criteria must be used with care. For example, consider an agency with a budget of $1000 and two mutually exclusive projects with the following characteristics to choose from:

Project	Discounted Benefits	Discounted Costs	B/C	Net Present Value
A	$ 200	$ 100	2.0	100
B	$1,500	$1,000	1.5	500.

Using the benefit-cost ratio criterion, project A appears preferable to project B, whereas application of the net present value approach suggests the opposite conclusion. Since only one of these projects can be undertaken, which should it be? This question is easily answered once the discounted costs and benefits of the projects are made comparable.

If project A is undertaken, the agency would have an additional $900 (the difference between the cost of projects B and A) to invest in other projects or perhaps return to the taxpayers. The issue of whether project A is preferred to B turns on how the agency uses the funds it would save by undertaking A rather than B. Suppose that the $900 could be employed in the next best alternative investment to yield discounted net benefits of $1000. We now have the information needed to make the projects comparable. Taking into account the auxiliary $900 investment if project A is adopted, we obtain the following amended set of characteristics:

Project	Discounted Benefits	Discounted Costs	B/C	Net Present Value
A (amended)	$1,200	$1,000	1.2	$200
B	$1,500	$1,000	1.5	$500.

Both criteria now agree. Once the projects have been made comparable, it becomes clear that project B in this example is the more efficient of the two.

The proof that both criteria will always agree—and thus that either may justifiably be used—once the projects have been made comparable in costs is relatively straightforward. Denote the discounted benefits and costs from projects A and B as B_a and C_a, and B_b and C_b, respectively. Suppose, for example, that $B_a - C_a > B_b - C_b$. If the projects have been made comparable so that $C_a = C_b$, then it follows from $(B_a - C_a)/C_a > (B_b - C_b)/C_a$ that $B_a/C_a > B_b/C_b$.

The above example demonstrates clearly some of the problems involved in determining the better of two projects. In practical applications, however, there can be many projects from which to choose. The same principles apply. With a budget constraint the goal is to choose that combination of projects that yields the highest net present value. As an example of this type of problem, consider an agency that has a budget of $285,000 and six projects (described in table 3–2) from which to choose. The projects have been arranged in descending order of benefit-cost ratios. The cumulative sum of net present value and of total costs are in the sixth and seventh columns of the table. *When the costs are similar,* this type of ranking can be quite useful in determining which projects to select given the budget constraint. Note that if the four projects with the highest benefit-cost ratios are selected, then the total expenditure will be $267,000 and the sum of the net present values is $608,000. No other project can be undertaken given the remaining funds and there is no way the net present value can be increased by dropping out any of the projects already included to make room for either project 5 or 6. For simplicity we rule out the possibility of using the remaining $18,000 for another project.

Unfortunately, this procedure, while it provides the correct answer in cases where costs are similar, does not always work. For example, suppose a seventh project (with the following characteristics) is added to the list of possibilities:

B_{PV}	C_{PV}	$B - C$	B/C
279	145	134	1.92.

If the budget remains the same, one might be tempted to reject this project since its benefit-cost ratio is lower than any of those already chosen. Notice however that if projects 3 and 4 are dropped and number 7 added, costs will fall by $129,000 due to the loss of 3 and 4 but go up by $145,000 due to the addition of project 7. This alteration will put total costs at $283,000, which is still within the budget constraint. More importantly there will be a net increase in the sum of the net present values (it falls by $131,000 when projects 3 and 4 are deleted but the addition of project 7 increases it by $134,000). Therefore, it is obvious that under these circumstances the optimal combination of projects is 1, 2, and 7, not 1, 2, 3, and 4.

The conclusions to draw from this example are as follows. The main economic efficiency goal when choosing projects subject to a budget constraint is to maximize net present value. In cases where the costs of the various projects

Table 3–2
Comparison of the Net Present Value and Benefit-Cost Ratio Criteria
(thousands of dollars)

Project	B_{PV}	C_{PV}	$B - C$	B/C	$\Sigma (B - C)$	ΣC
1	357	70	287	5.10	287	70
2	258	68	190	3.79	477	138
3	160	79	81	2.03	558	217
4	100	50	50	2.00	608	267
5	90	53	37	1.69	645	320
6	70	47	23	1.48	668	367

are similar, the benefit-cost ratios can be helpful in determining the proper combination. In many cases, however, a trial and error method of choosing the various combinations that are possible given the budget constraint, and then comparing the net present value that results, is preferable. This points up the fact that net present value is the most generally useful benefit-cost criterion. The internal rate of return is difficult to derive and can be ambiguous. The benefit-cost ratio, while useful in determining if a project passes the basic Hicks-Kaldor criteria, is only marginally useful in making comparisons between projects. It is not, however, inconsistent with net present value as a ranking device if costs are made similar through comparisons of alternative investments.

Summary

We have discussed the conventional method of accounting for time streams of benefits and costs. In this section we briefly summarize the main points made in the chapter.

Discounting Future Effects

Benefits and costs occurring at one point in time (say, the present) are not directly comparable to benefits and costs occurring at some other point in time. The technique for making benefits and costs which occur at various times commensurable is *discounting,* that is, the translation of future values into present values. In particular, the total present value of a time stream of benefits (B_{PV}) is defined as:

$$B_{PV} = B_0 + \frac{B_1}{(1 + r)} + \frac{B_2}{(1 + r)^2} + \ldots + \frac{B_N}{(1 + r)^N},$$

where r is the discount rate and B_i is the estimated benefit for the ith year. Similarly, the total present value of a time stream of costs (C_{PV}) is defined as:

$$C_{PV} = C_0 + \frac{C_1}{(1+r)} + \frac{C_2}{(1+r)^2} + \ldots + \frac{C_N}{(1+r)^N} .$$

Selection of the Discount Rate

While there is controversy among economists over the exact set of criteria to be employed in selecting a discount rate, the benefit-cost analyst cannot await the resolution of theoretic disputes—the analyst must select a discount rate. For reasons set forth above, we recommend using as the discount rate for public sector projects a measure of the consumption and investment opportunities that will be foregone in the private sector as a result of higher taxes or more government borrowing. In particular this opportunity cost measure is a weighted average rate of return to private sector activities (r_p):

$$r_p = w_1 r_1 + w_2 r_2 + \ldots + w_j r_j + \ldots + w_J r_J$$

where w_j is the share of funds coming from the jth sector of the economy and r_j is the rate of return available in the jth sector. Earlier studies have found r_p to be around 7 to 8 percent; however, this range may no longer be appropriate. Many governmental agencies use discount rates in the 10 to 15 percent range. In any event, the analyst should discount all time streams with some alternative discount rates in order to test the sensitivity of a study's findings to changes in the discount rate employed.

Alternative Benefit-Cost Criteria

In judging the desirability (in an efficiency sense) of various public sector projects there are three alternative criteria: (1) net present value, (2) benefit-cost ratios, and (3) internal rate of return. In some circumstances, projects will have multiple internal rates of return and in such cases there are inherent ambiguities associated with the application of the internal rate-of-return criterion. Consequently, the other two decision criteria are preferable for benefit-cost studies. In general, the net present value approach is more useful than the benefit-cost ratio approach, but both can be of use provided the analyst keeps in mind the principle that economic efficiency considerations ultimately require government agencies to maximize discounted net benefits (rather than a ratio of benefits to costs).

4

Other Issues in the Measurement of Benefits and Costs

In this chapter we address three additional important issues in connection with the measurement of benefits and costs. First, we discuss alternative techniques for considering the uncertainty that necessarily surrounds many of the benefit-cost effects, particularly those that will occur some years in the future. Second, we discuss the role of income-distributional equity in benefit-cost analyses and consider the types of effects that should be measured in assessing a project's distributional impact. Finally, we address the problem of intangibles, that is, those effects that, while potentially very important, remain unquantified.

Risk and Uncertainty

The essence of benefit-cost analysis is the identification and measurement of a project's benefits and costs. Normally, a program's effects are experienced over some period of time, so there are naturally uncertainties or risks associated with any attempt to predict the precise magnitude of those effects. The measurement of benefits and costs in effect requires the analyst to predict—perhaps over very long periods of time—such things as changes in consumption patterns, population movements and trends, technological discoveries, and perhaps even weather patterns. In this section we discuss a number of alternative approaches to handling the problems posed by uncertain or risky outcomes. Economists commonly distinguish between risk and uncertainty. *Risk* refers to situations in which information about the probability of an outcome's occurrence is available, whereas *uncertainty* refers to situations where there is no such information.

Before discussing the details of this problem one further point is in order. Just because we cannot know for certain all of the effects of a project nor how these effects may be translated into willingness to pay, it does not mean that benefit-cost analysis is of no value. Uncertainty about the future is an inherent aspect of living. Decisions have to be made with the best information available. The role of the benefit-cost analyst in this regard is to provide the best estimates he can obtain, and when necessary acknowledge any uncertainties and perform one or more of the analyses to be described below so that the decisionmaker can know the ramifications of having less-than-perfect knowledge.

Cut-Off Period

One approach to dealing with risky or uncertain outcomes is to adopt some arbitrary cut-off (or pay-back) period. In the case of extremely risky projects the cut-off period might be as short as two or three years; in other cases it might be as long as thirty to fifty years. This strategy toward handling risk or uncertainty would result in the adoption of only those projects capable of generating (discounted) benefits prior to the cut-off sufficient to more than cover (discounted) project costs. This decision rule, which is analogous to the pay-back criteria commonly employed by businessmen in judging the desirability of private investments, implicitly assumes that the risk or uncertainty associated with benefits and costs expected to occur past the cut-off date is so great that the analyst is justified in simply ignoring those effects. Extremely short cut-off periods such as two or three years would seldom appear justified in evaluating public projects. Analyses conducted with short cut-off periods ignore all information related to periods past the cut-off. Even when there is considerable uncertainty about the magnitudes of future effects, the analyst would probably be well-advised to avoid discarding or ignoring potentially useful information simply because it applies to periods past the cut-off.

Relatively long cut-off periods such as 50 or 100 years are more justifiable than very short periods. The longer the period of time involved (other things equal), the greater is the degree of uncertainty; we can be much more confident, for instance, about predicting consumption patterns 5 years hence than in predicting such patterns 50 years from now. Moreover, as we noted in chapter 3, discounting tends to render effects occurring so far in the future relatively unimportant, so ignoring them may be justifiable in many circumstances. Benefit-cost analysts commonly adopt cut-off periods of 50 to 100 years since the present value of such distant effects tends to be relatively small. This strategy arises more out of computational convenience than out of an attempt to cope with risk or uncertainty, however.

Discount Rate Adjustments

An alternative approach to coping with the problem of uncertainty involves arbitrary adjustments to the discount rate. So as to err on the conservative side, the adjustments commonly entail increases in the rate used to discount benefits and decreases in the discount rate applied to costs. These alternatives tend to reduce the magnitude of discounted benefits while increasing that of discounted costs. Consequently, they tend to result in fewer projects being adopted on economic efficiency grounds.

This procedure is probably preferable to the adoption of a cut-off period since it discounts, rather than completely discards, information about future benefits and costs. Nevertheless, it too involves highly arbitrary decisions and, thus, should generally be avoided in favor of other techniques for handling risk and uncertainty. The analyst must decide not only which portion of the time stream of benefits and costs should be discounted with the adjusted discount rates, but also what the magnitudes of the adjustments should be. One method of reducing the arbitrariness in the selection of the adjustment magnitude has been suggested by Arrow and Lind (1970). They suggest examining the rates of return being earned on similar investments in the private sector to determine the appropriate adjustment magnitudes. For instance, if private sector projects of a particular variety, say hydroelectric plants, are yielding a 15 percent rate of return whereas the overall opportunity cost of capital is 10 percent, then the appropriate adjustment magnitude would be 5 percent (i.e., the difference between the two rates). That is, in this instance it would be natural to discount future effects from public hydroelectric projects with a rate of 15 percent.

Expected Values

Another approach to explicitly introducing risk considerations into a benefit-cost analysis is to treat estimated benefits and costs as random variables that can be described by some probability distribution. Suppose, for instance, that an analysis of historical flood patterns suggests that the discounted benefits from a flood-control project will range from zero (if no flood occurs) to $100 million (if the worst possible flood occurs); the same analysis would also reveal the probability that a flood of any given severity would occur. Suppose for illustrative purposes that we can identify only four possible outcomes along with the probability that any given outcome will occur. (In practice the number of alternative outcomes is likely to be much larger than the number used here.) This information could then be summarized as:

Value of Discounted Benefits	Probability of Occurrence
$0	0.3
$30 million	0.4
$50 million	0.2
$100 million	0.1

Which of these discounted values, or which combination of values, should be used in computing this project's benefit-cost ratio or net present value? The conventional method of arriving at one unique value when this type of information is available is to calculate the project's *expected value,* which is a weighted average of the alternative outcomes:

$$\text{Expected Value of Benefits} = (\$0 \times 0.3) + (\$30 \text{ million} \times 0.4)$$
$$+ (\$50 \text{ million} \times 0.2)$$
$$+ (\$100 \text{ million} \times 0.1)$$
$$= \$32 \text{ million}.$$

Suppose that the discounted cost of this flood control project is $31 million. Should this project be undertaken? An examination of the probability distribution of benefits reveals that there is a 70 percent chance the actual benefits will be less than the $31 million project cost. Nevertheless, the project should probably be undertaken because the expected value calculation indicates that the *average* benefit from such projects will be $32 million. That is, if ten such projects were undertaken we could, on average, expect no benefits from three of them, $30 million in benefits from each of four projects, $50 million each from two projects, and $100 million from one, for an average benefit of $32 million.

This example introduced risk into the analysis by treating the discounted benefits as a random variable. In practice, it is likely that each estimated annual benefit and cost will be a random variable, suggesting that the appropriate discounting procedure (when information about probability distributions is available) is to translate *expected* future benefits, $E(B)$, and costs $E(C)$, into an expected present value, $E(PV)$. For example, the proper treatment of benefits would be:

$$E(PV \text{ of benefits}) = E(B_0) + \frac{E(B_1)}{1+r} + \frac{E(B_2)}{(1+r)^2} + \ldots + \frac{E(B_n)}{(1+r)^n},$$

where $E(B_i)$ is the expected value of the benefits for the ith year.

One serious problem with these expected value calculations is that they take into account only the *mean* or average value of the distribution, ignoring other potentially important characteristics of a distribution such as the variance. For instance, consider two mutually exclusive equal-cost projects, each offering expected discounted benefits of $10 million. Should the analyst recommend that these projects are equally desirable on efficiency grounds? Probably not, unless the benefit distributions of these two projects are quite similar. Suppose, for example, that two projects (A and B) have benefit distributions such as:

Project A		Project B	
Benefit Distribution	*Probability of Occurrence*	*Benefit Distribution*	*Probability of Occurrence*
$10 million	1.0	$0	0.9
		$100 million	0.1

Both project have the same expected value of $10 million; however, they have substantially different benefit distributions. In the present example, as long as decisionmakers are at all risk averse, they will clearly prefer project A (other things equal) with its certain gain of $10 million to project B, which offers only a small chance of enjoying a very large gain.

Another difficulty with relying upon this approach to handling risk is the difficulty and the cost of discovering the nature of the necessary probability distributions. While the probabilities of some events (for example, floods and hurricanes) may be easily obtained from historical records, the probability distributions for many other variables (for example, input and output prices) may be exceedingly difficult and costly to obtain.

Game Theory: Maximin Strategy

In the absence of reliable information about probability distributions, it will sometimes prove useful to apply game theory techniques in evaluating alternative public sector projects. One such approach or technique is the *maximin* strategy, which refers to *maximizing the minimum.* This approach to evaluating outcomes is an extremely conservative one that implicitly assumes that the worst possible outcomes always occur.

To illustrate this technique, we assume the analyst is evaluating three mutually exclusive, equal-cost flood control projects (A, B, and C) that would generate discounted benefits of $100 million, $120 million, and $150 million, respectively, if severe flooding occurs. If no flooding occurs, the projects still yield discounted benefits (for example, recreational or irrigational) in the respective amounts of $30 million, $60 million, and $20 million. (For simplicity we assume only two possible events, either severe flooding or no flooding whatsoever.) No reliable information is available regarding the probability of the flood occurring.

The various possible outcomes can be illustrated in the following simple matrix:

	Severe Flooding	No Flooding
Project A	$100 million	$30 million
Project B	$120 million	$60 million
Project C	$150 million	$20 million

The maximin strategy indicates that project B is preferable to projects A and C on the grounds that B provides a minimum benefit of $60 million versus $30 million and $20 million for projects A and C, respectively. That is, the selection of B would maximize the minimum gain from undertaking a flood control project.

Unfortunately, in many instances this conservative maximin criterion will lead to the rejection of the more preferable projects. Suppose for instance that the above benefit matrix were altered in the following fashion:

	Severe Flooding	*No Flooding*
Project A	$700 million	$49 million
Project B	$150 million	$50 million
Project C	$800 million	$48 million

Under these revised circumstances, the maximin criterion still recommends project B even though it is now almost certainly inferior to either project A or C. The problem with the maximin strategy is essentially the same as the problem with the cut-off period criterion—it ignores potentially useful information, namely, all gains other than the minimum gain.

Game Theory: Minimax-Regret

An alternative game theoretic approach is the *minimax-regret* criteria, that is, minimizing the maximum regret or loss that might occur. The minimax-regret strategy more fully utilizes the available information about possible future outcomes than does the maximin approach.

The minimax-regret criteria is easily illustrated with the aid of the example presented in the preceding benefit matrix. Suppose that severe flooding does, in fact, occur. In that event, project C would have provided the greatest advantage ($800 million in benefits). Had project A been undertaken, rather than project C, the foregone benefits from not undertaking C would be $100 million ($800 million − $700 million). Likewise, had project B been undertaken, rather than project C, the foregone benefits would be $650 million ($800 million − $150 million). On the other hand, if we suppose that no flooding occurs, project B generates the most benefits, namely, $50 million. If projects A or C are selected (and no flood occurs), the foregone benefits from failing to undertake project B would be $1 million and $2 million, respectively. This information can also be presented in matrix form:

	Severe Flood	No Flood	Row Maximum
Project A	$100 million	$1 million	$100 million
Project B	$650 million	$0	$650 million
Project C	$0	$2 million	$2 million

The matrix can be interpreted as follows. If project B is adopted and there is no flood, there is no "regret" in the sense that another project would have yielded higher net benefits. On the other hand, if project A is chosen and no flood occurs, there is a $1 million regret for not undertaking project B. Examination of the various row maximums indicates that selection of project A might cause us to forego $100 million in benefits, selection of project B entails a potential opportunity cost of $650 million, whereas selection of project C involves a maximum regret of $2 million. The minimax-regret strategy would lead the analyst to recommend project C, since the worst the policymaker could do by selecting C would be to forego (in the event of no flood) an extra $2 million offered by project B.

In cases of uncertainty, it may be prudent to do both a maximin and a minimax-regret on the data. Both provide useful information, and only the decisionmaker knows which will be the best strategy for him.

Sensitivity Analysis

Another approach to handling risk and uncertainty—one that should be used in conjunction with the preceding methods—is the application of sensitivity analysis. The analyst can have far more confidence in predicting that some variable (say, benefit or cost) will fall within a certain range (say, between $10 million to $100 million) than in predicting a precise value for that variable. Consequently, whenever there is considerable uncertainty about the reliability of a predicted benefit or cost, the analyst should recalculate the benefit-cost ratios or net present values for some alternative values, presumably upper and lower bound estimates of the variable in question. An advantage of this approach to coping with risk or uncertainty is that it allows the analyst to identify those (uncertain) estimates that are crucial to the analysis. If the sensitivity analysis reveals that even relatively large changes in a particular estimate do not alter the general outcome of the study, the fact that some risk or uncertainty may surround that estimate is unimportant. This issue of sensitivity analysis is taken up in greater detail and illustrated in chapter 5.

Summary

In this section we have discussed a number of alternative techniques for dealing with risky or uncertain outcomes in benefit-cost analyses. We considered the following topics: (1) use of cut-off periods, (2) discount rate adjustments, (3) calculation of expected values, (4) use of the maximin criteria, and (5) application of the minimax-regret criteria. In addition, we considered the use of sensitivity analysis in connection with all of these techniques for handling risk or uncertainty. Short cut-off periods are rarely used by benefit-cost analysts; they ignore too much potentially valuable information about future effects. Longer cut-off periods of 50 to 100 years are commonly employed in benefit-cost studies but more as a computational convenience than as a means of coping with risk or uncertainty. Discount rate adjustments can be made so as to put less weight on distant benefits and more weight on future costs; such adjustments would reduce the number of projects acceptable under economic efficiency criteria. This approach can be somewhat arbitrary and in addition may put too large a burden on the discount rate. The expected value approach is the conventional method for dealing with risk; however, it does demand the use of explicit probability distributions and these may be costly and difficult to estimate. In the absence of information about probability distributions, the maximin criteria and the minimax-regret criteria provide alternative techniques for coping with uncertainty.

It is frequently the case, however, that benefit-cost analysts do not introduce risk or uncertainty elements into the analysis in quite so formal a fashion as that described in much of this chapter. Uncertainty about future benefits or costs is often taken into account through the simple expedient of sensitivity analysis.

Distributional Considerations

Benefit-cost analysis as we have described it focuses on the economic efficiency aspects of government activities; that is, on the identification and measurement of the real benefits and costs of such activities. This basis for efficiency comparisons is the Hicks-Kaldor criterion that the gains to "winners" are large enough to allow for potential compensation to "losers" and still leave a net increase in the value of production for the gainers. The word *potential* is critical. It is entirely possible that a project that has a positive net present value will result in some very large negative effects on some individuals or groups. Policymakers would surely want to be apprised of such things. In a more general sense, they are interested in the distributional aspects of a project as well as the economic efficiency aspects. In fact, in many instances the distributional considerations may be of overriding importance from a policy standpoint. Consequently, it will usually be desirable for the analyst to indicate, to the extent feasible, how the benefits and costs of a proposed project are likely to be distributed across the relevant classes of people.

While there are numerous classifications that may be used in accounting for distributional effects, the more familiar ones include income, race, sex, age, region (or neighborhood), religion, family size, occupation, and educational background. Of course, each of these characteristics could be finely subdivided.

Unfortunately, in addition to the difficulties and costs associated with estimating how the benefits and costs are actually distributed, the mere presentation of this information can be difficult to accomplish even for a relatively few classifications. For instance, describing the distributional effects of a project across ten income groups, eight age classes, four racial categories, and six regions requires a table (or tables) containing nearly 2,000 separate cells. Unless most of the cells in such a large table were empty, most readers would probably find it very difficult to digest that much detail. Consequently, while distributional effects may be of considerable interest, the cost of identifying and measuring such effects and the problems associated with transmitting highly detailed information suggest the analyst should normally work with relatively broad classifications.

In some instances, policymakers will have definite preferences for specific types of distributional information, in which case the analyst need be concerned only with the measurement problems. Frequently, however, the analyst will be left with considerable discretion over what, if any, information about the distribution of benefits and costs is presented.

One way of conveniently organizing some reasonably detailed results of a distributional investigation is illustrated in table 4–1. (The same general format has been recommended by Weisbrod (1966).) This type of table provides for the presentation of information regarding a program's distributional consequences in terms of income, age, race, and region. Of course, it can easily be altered to include additional variables (say, sex) or to substitute one variable for another. The use of this type of table is illustrated in chapter 5.

Ideally, distributional measures should reflect all changes in economic welfare (for example, income or wealth changes) occasioned by a government program, not just those changes associated with the real (efficiency) benefits and costs. Alterations in a family's economic position can be caused as easily through purely pecuniary effects such as price or tax changes (which should be ignored in assessing a program's efficiency) as by real effects, and such effects should consequently be taken into account if possible when assessing a program's distributional impact. Thus, an assessment of distributional impacts should in principle take into account both the real effects and all of the pecuniary and secondary effects of a project.

Usually the analyst's contribution in this area is limited to the identification and measurement of a program's distributional effects. Of course, this statement

Table 4–1
Distribution of Net Benefits by Income, Age, Race, and Region of Beneficiary

Region and Age Group	Income Class						
	$0–$4,999		$5,000–$14,000		$15,000 and above		
	White	Nonwhite	White	Nonwhite	White	Nonwhite	Total
Northeast							
0 to 18 years							
19 to 64 years							
65 years and above							
North Central							
0 to 18 years							
19 to 64 years							
65 years and above							
South							
0 to 18 years							
19 to 64 years							
65 years and above							
West							
0 to 18 years							
19 to 64 years							
65 years and above							
Total							

should not be interpreted as implying that this task is easily accomplished; on the contrary, in many instances it will be exceedingly difficult and costly to obtain accurate estimates of a program's distributional consequences. It is common for distributional assessments to be limited to simply identifying whether particular groups are gainers or losers, with no serious effort being made to measure the magnitude of a program's distributional consequences.

However, in principle the integration of the distributional effects into the benefit-cost study can be carried much further than the identification or measurement stages. Conceptually, we can treat the desirable distributional effects of a program as a social benefit, just as we treat a program's desirable efficiency effects; the undesirable distributional consequences can, of course, be similarly viewed as social costs. To do this, the analyst could assign weights (determined perhaps by a legislature) to distributional gains and losses so as to make them comparable both across groups and also with efficiency gains and losses. To illustrate this point, consider a program that would confer real discounted benefits of $1 million to group A while imposing $2 million in real discounted costs on group B. (For simplicity we ignore all distributional changes associated with secondary or pecuniary effects.) On strict benefit-cost efficiency grounds, this project should be rejected since its net present value ($NPV = B - C$) is negative. This decision rule implicitly treats a dollar gain, or loss, the same regardless of the group involved. Suppose, however, that social (legislative?) objectives suggested that a dollar gain (or loss) to group A should receive three times the weight received by a similar gain (or loss) to group B. In light of such information, we would have to revalue the gains to group A at $3 million ($1 million X 3), thereby making the project desirable on "grand" benefit-cost grounds, that is, once the distributional gains are taken into account. Unfortunately, the analyst will rarely have such explicit distributional weights available and, thus, may be restricted to simply presenting estimates of a program's distributional effects to policymakers.

When an analyst is certain that distributional effects are of central importance to the decisionmaker, he can attempt to provide information on the trade-offs between economic efficiency and distributional gains. Suppose one social goal is to redistribute income to a certain minority group, but there is a hesitancy to provide an explicit distributional weighting scheme. In this situation the projects that are accepted by any agency will tend to favor this group. It should be remembered, however, that meeting this social goal will have its cost in terms of lost economic efficiency. To make this point explicit, the analyst can provide a list of the project groupings which are possible given the agency's budget constraint, but which have different efficiency and distributional aspects. Such a list is provided in the following hypothetical example:

Project Grouping	NPV	Gains to Minority Group
A	$100,000	$20,000
B	$ 90,000	$25,000
C	$ 80,000	$29,000
D	$ 70,000	$32,000
E	$ 60,000	$34,000

Project group A is the one that would be chosen on pure efficiency grounds. It has an NPV of $100,000 and it also generates gains to the minority group of $20,000, where these gains may include direct and secondary effects. If project group B is chosen NPV falls to $90,000 but gains to the minority group increase to $25,000. Similarly, project groups C, D, and E can provide increases in minority gains at the expense of NPV. Notice that the trade-off is becoming less and less favorable. That is, the change from B to C results in an increase of

$4,000 to the minority group for a loss of $10,000 in NPV, but going from C to D will only generate a $3,000 gain for the same loss in NPV.

By presenting this type of information to decisionmakers they will have some notion of what distributional gains are costing society in terms of efficiency. While they may agree that the distributional effects are desirable and they may be willing to accept the sacrifice implicit in the move from A to C to achieve some distributional gains, they may determine that a further change from C to D may be too expensive for the gains achieved.

Allowance for Intangible Effects

It is commonly the case that certain efficiency or distributional effects, although perhaps quite important, must remain unmeasured (or be measured very imperfectly) because of incomplete data or the absence of commonly accepted measurement techniques. We refer to such unmeasured or unmeasurable effects as *intangible* benefits or costs. As an illustration of intangible effects, Weisbrod (1965) pointed out—but was unable to measure—a number of benefits from programs designed to prevent high school dropouts. Included among the intangible benefits of such programs were improved self-esteem of students, increased social and political consciousness, and reductions in the incidence of crime and delinquency. In principle, we recognize such effects as being potentially important results of dropout prevention programs; however, in practice it is not possible to obtain estimates of willingness to pay for them given existing methodologies.

When confronted with the problem of dealing with intangible benefits or costs what can the analyst do? At a minimum, the analyst should clearly identify all intangible benefits and costs. In some instances it will not be possible to do more than list the types of effects as in the example of the high school dropout reduction program. In other cases, however, it may be possible to denote some sort of physical measurement as well. For instance, in addition to electricity a nuclear power plant produces heated water and radioactive wastes. If there is a lack of adequate knowledge of the local ecology and how it relates to the economy, the effects of these outputs represent an intangible for purposes of the benefit-cost analysis. It may be useful, however, to describe exactly how much heated water or radioactive wastes will be discharged at what locations and over what periods of time. These unmeasured effects can sometimes be far more important than the quantified effects and, consequently, must not be overlooked by the analyst or the policymaker.

One way to incorporate intangible effects into a benefit-cost analysis—other than merely identifying them—is to answer the following question. Does it appear likely in any particular instance that the values affected by the intangible effects could have been large enough, if they had in fact been quantified, to have substantially altered the findings of the benefit-cost study? To illustrate this approach, consider a hypothetical lifesaving program that could save 1,000 lives a year at a cost of $100,000 per life (assume constant marginal costs for simplicity). Suppose it is estimated that the discounted productivity gains to society, if these lives are saved, would average $75,000 per life, but that no estimate of the individual aspects of saving lives can be made (see chapter 2).

The measured social costs of this program ($100,000 per life) clearly exceed the measured social benefits ($75,000 per life). Should the analyst recommend, on efficiency grounds, that the program be rejected? Since the social value of a person's life is, as was pointed out above, greater than the discounted value of what that person can be expected to contribute to the gross national product, the program should be rejected on efficiency grounds only if the intangible benefits of saving a life are presumed to be less than $25,000, the difference between the measured costs and benefits. Since the analyst may not be able to measure the individual aspects of saving a life, a useful approach would be to inform policymakers as to (1) which effects have not been measured and (2) the magnitudes that would have to be attained by the intangible effects ($25,000 in this example) before they could alter the conclusion implied by the measured effects. In the above example this would involve informing the decisionmaker that 1,000 lives would be saved and if the individual (or nonproductive) aspects of each life saved are worth $25,000 or more on average, the project makes sense on efficiency grounds. This will provide information on the trade-offs involved. Of course, the decisionmaker's dilemma is relatively easy to resolve when the required value of a life need only be $100: the project should be undertaken. However, if it must be $5 billion per life, then the project more than likely should not be undertaken.

This approach demonstrates the fact that intangible effects, regardless of their true magnitude, may be relatively unimportant to the benefit-cost analyst or the policymaker under certain circumstances. Suppose that in the preceding example the estimated discounted benefits of saving a life exceeded the discounted costs, and that the only issue involved was whether to undertake a program of a given size. In this instance, the fact that there may be substantial unmeasured benefits associated with the program is unimportant (unless a budget constraint prevents the agency from undertaking all efficiency-enhancing programs) because the benefits that can be measured exceed the costs. Of course, if the size of the program is open to question, then the intangible effects would still be relevant. Economic efficiency requires that programs should be expanded until the social marginal benefits of the program just equal the program's social marginal costs and the presence of intangibles makes it impossible to know the precise point at which this equality is attained.

If there is some positive probability that the intangible effects will, in fact, not occur, then the analyst (and decisionmakers) must be concerned with making judgments about the possible expected values of the intangible effects.

To illustrate, suppose that the measured net discounted benefits (discounted benefits minus discounted costs) of a certain water development project equal $10 million. Suppose further that there is one chance out of four that some adverse but intangible environmental effects may result from the project. The question the analyst must address is whether the expected value of the intangible costs, $E(IC)$, is likely to exceed the $10 million in net measured benefits. Since the expected value of an effect is defined as the probability, p, of the effect occurring times the value of the effect, IC, were it to actually occur, we can write:

$$E(IC) = p \times IC.$$

In the present example since $p = .25$, trying to determine whether $E(IC) > \$10$ million is the same as trying to make a judgment as to whether $IC > \$40$ million. (See chapter 3 for additional discussion of expected values.) As long as the analyst takes into account the fact that the intangible effect only has some probability of occurring, it is irrelevant whether the judgmental effort focuses on IC or $E(IC)$.

It will often be the case however that the analyst and the decisionmakers will be confronted with two unknown parameters in connection with intangibles: (1) the value of the intangible effects themselves and (2) the probability that those effects will, in fact, occur. Thus, judgments must be made about the components of the expected value, that is, about both p and IC.

A way to approach this problem that has been used by Crutchfield and Stokes (1973) is illustrated in figure 4–1. The *iso-value* curve in figure 4–1 shows all the combinations of p and IC that would result in the expected value of the intangible effects ($p \times IC$) exactly equaling a project's net discounted benefits, which in the present example is taken to be $10 million. For instance, point A on the curve corresponds to $p = 0.5$ and $IC = \$20$ million, so $E(IC) = \$10$ million. Likewise, point B corresponds to $p = 1.0$ and $IC = \$10$ million, resulting again in $E(IC) = \$10$ million. All points to the left or below this iso-value curve (for example, point D) correspond to combinations of p and IC that would result in expected values less than the critical value of $10 million (in the present example). Conversely, all points above or to the right of the iso-value curve (for example, point C) reflect combinations of p and IC consistent with expected values greater than the critical level.

In this type of situation, the analyst and, ultimately, the policymakers must make a judgment about which combination of p and IC seems plausible. If the more plausible combinations lie below the iso-value curve, then the project should be undertaken (on efficiency grounds). On the other hand, if the more plausible combinations seem to lie above the iso-value curve, then the expected intangible costs are so large relative to the measured discounted net benefits that the project should probably be rejected on efficiency grounds.

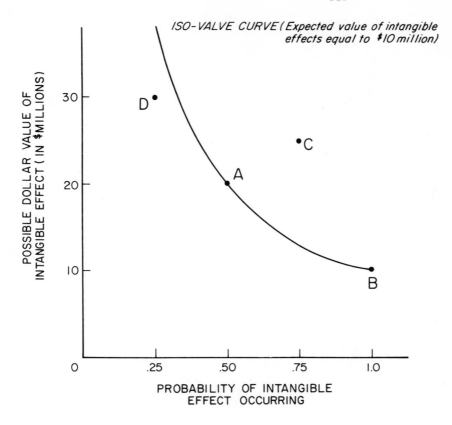

Figure 4-1. Intangible Effects and Iso-Value Curves

It should be made clear that the selection of which combinations of *p* and *IC* appear to be plausible may involve little more than educated guesses. Intangibles, by definition, are those effects that were not quantifiable through the application of conventional economic measurement techniques. Thus, the assignment of probable values to intangibles is almost certainly going to involve a considerable amount of guesswork. At a minimum, the analyst should clearly indicate which judgments are based largely upon such guesswork.

5   The Benefit-Cost Report

This chapter discusses the presentation of findings of a benefit-cost study. The form taken by the benefit-cost report and the manner in which the results are presented are very important, since the benefit-cost report serves as the primary, if not the only, means of conveying the study's findings to policy-makers. Unless care is taken in the preparation of the benefit-cost report, valuable information about assumptions crucial to the study may be overlooked or misunderstood by policymakers. There are no doubt a number of effective formats an analyst could use in developing a benefit-cost report, however, they should all ultimately convey essentially the same information. We find the format discussed below to be a useful one for conveying the relevant information generated by the benefit-cost study and consequently strongly urge the analyst to use this (or a similar) approach in communicating the results of benefit-cost analyses. In general, a benefit-cost report should include, at a minimum, the following information:

1. A description of the program objectives and accounting stance,
2. A taxonomy of direct benefits and costs and any noncanceling secondary effects,
3. A discussion of the effects for which benefit and cost estimates were actually made and of the methodology and data used in the measurements,
4. A display of the benefit-cost measures,
5. A discussion of the unmeasured and unmeasurable (intangible) effects and how they might be expected to alter the benefit-cost measures, and
6. A discussion of the distributional aspects of the project.

In the following sections we discuss in more complete terms these steps in a benefit-cost report and illustrate our recommended approach within the context of an actual benefit-cost study.

Program Objectives and the Accounting Stance

The first step in writing the benefit-cost report is to clearly identify the objectives of the program being analyzed and relate those objectives to the accounting stance employed in the study (see chapter 2 for further discussion of the accounting stance issue). The relationship between the program objectives and a

115

benefit-cost study's accounting stance becomes extremely important if there is some divergence between the two. For instance, consider a program designed to enhance regional development. Presumably, officials would be primarily interested in whether the regional benefits exceed the regional costs and perhaps only secondarily interested (if at all) in the program's nationwide efficiency implications. Consequently, the analyst should make explicit whether the study's accounting stance in this instance is regional or nationwide in nature.

It will sometimes be very difficult to identify program objectives—at least not with a high degree of certainty—because policymakers may have failed to clearly identify those objectives or because the objectives are seen differently by different policymakers. Nevertheless, the analyst will always be able to, and should, carefully specify the viewpoint, or accounting stance, taken in the benefit-cost study, thereby providing policymakers with the information necessary to interpret and judge the study's findings.

A Taxonomy of Benefit and Costs

The next step in the writing of the benefit-cost report is the identification of the various benefits and costs that should, on efficiency grounds, be taken into account and, where feasible, quantified. In more precise terms, the second step should be to provide a list of the direct outputs (both positive and negative) of the project and of the things that must be foregone to undertake it. The purpose of such an exhaustive taxonomy is to provide a benchmark for assessing the analyst's success in measuring the program's benefits and costs. Frequently, only some of those effects contained in this taxonomy will be amenable to quantification, given the present state of benefit-cost analysis. Nevertheless, it remains important to identify all benefits and costs so as to place those that are quantifiable into perspective. Ideally, we would like our measures of a program's gross benefits to capture all of those elements which, in combination, equal the sum of the willingness to pay of all individuals for a program's outputs or advantages; similarly, the taxonomy of social costs should capture all those elements which, in combination, equal the sum of the willingness to pay of all individuals to avoid a program's disadvantages. In line with our discussion of the general equilibrium approach and the partial equilibrium approach, a taxonomy of the direct outputs and direct costs will not adequately measure total social benefits and costs if there are secondary effects that do not cancel out. Therefore, if this is a relevant consideration, these noncanceling secondary effects should be added to the taxonomy.

To illustrate these points, we consider their application in a specific benefit-cost study. For illustrative purposes, we consider the problem of evaluating the efficiency implications of federal occupational safety and health (OSH) regulations. What are the social benefits and costs of such regulations? In addressing this question and developing the taxonomy, we first take up benefits and then turn to a consideration of costs.

A Taxonomy of Benefits: An Illustration.

1. One obvious efficiency gain from OSH improvements is the increase in present and future *market* productivity by those who, in the absence of governmental OSH regulation, would have had their productivity temporarily or permanently reduced (as in the case of death) by a job-related injury or illness. In principle, these productivity measures encompass all those who would have been disabled in the absence of government OSH standards, including nonworkers or third parties to whom work hazards represent an externality.

2. A related efficiency gain from an effective OSH standard is the increase in present and future *nonmarket* productivity (for example, in do-it-yourself activities) among those who would have otherwise been disabled or killed.

3. Another component of social willingness to pay for improved OSH is the value of the resources that otherwise would have been used in the detection, treatment, and rehabilitation of work hazard victims.

4. Reductions in work-related injuries and illnesses may also be valued for the resources released from the administration of workmen's compensation and other insurance.

5. Job-related disabilities may occasion the training of personnel to replace those disabled. To the extent that OSH improvements reduce the need for replacement personnel, these training resources would be freed for alternative uses and, thus, should be accounted for in an approximation of social willingness to pay for better OSH.

6. The presence of OSH hazards may lead to avoidance efforts and expenditures by workers or employers. OSH standards specifying the precise manner in which a hazard is to be reduced or eliminated may well substitute for such private efforts, thereby freeing additional private resources for alternative uses and perhaps making workers, who now need to expend less effort at being cautious, more productive.

7. Another form of benefit from OSH standards is the reduction in losses arising from the pain and suffering attendant in work-related injuries and illnesses and risk aversion among those who stand to suffer a probabilistic loss from work hazards.

8. OSH standards may also benefit owners of capital inasmuch as they prevent or reduce damage not only to workers, but also to the stock of capital (for example, machinery or buildings).

9. Finally, governmental efforts to reduce work hazards may confer benefits on the firm since the improvements in OSH may reduce absenteeism and work

stoppages or slowdowns and, possibly, improve the overall morale and productivity of the work force.

A Taxonomy of Social Costs: An Illustration.

In this section we identify a number of efficiency costs likely to accompany the imposition of effective OSH standards. It is these social costs which, in principle, must be offset against the social benefits noted above to determine whether any particular standard is desirable on efficiency grounds.

1. One obvious social cost occasioned by OSH regulations is the cost of compliance, that is, the present and future real resource expenditures necessitated by law.

2. Additional resources will be expended on the establishment and enforcement of OSH regulations. This category includes not only government expenditures, but also private sector expenditures related to the establishment and enforcement of OSH regulations. For instance, labor unions may expend resources in efforts to make their views known as regards, say, the proposed stringency of a particular standard, and such expenditures should in principle be taken into account.

3. To the extent that OSH standards lead to higher prices for goods and services, there may be a dead-weight loss of consumers' surplus (see chapter 2). This loss constitutes a real social cost and therefore must be included in our taxonomy and, if feasible, quantified.

4. Finally, OSH standards may give rise to some resource unemployment, which implies lost output. Thus, the extent and duration of resource unemployment occasioned by an OSH standard must also be taken into account when assessing the social costs of the regulation.

This completes the illustrative taxonomy of benefits and costs occasioned by OSH standards. In an actual benefit-cost study the analyst would probably want to explain the economic rationale for each benefit and cost in somewhat greater detail than we employed in the preceding example. Our discussion was abbreviated in order to keep the illustration to manageable proportions. Nonetheless, the length and the makeup of the list help make an important point. While it is obvious that all points on the list are direct effects of the project, most readers will have to admit, if asked to make such a list, that they probably would have failed to include one or more of them. Government programs and projects have far ranging direct effects, some of which are not apparent from an initial examination of the problem. But to do a proper benefit-cost analysis, all effects must be considered. Therefore, the construction of the taxonomy must be done with great care.

Benefit-Cost Measurements

Once the taxonomy of benefits and costs has been developed, the next step in writing the benefit-cost report is a detailed explanation of the techniques and data used in measuring those effects that were in fact quantifiable. Emphasis should be given in this part of the report to justifying, or at least highlighting, the more restrictive and controversial assumptions made in constructing benefit-cost measures. In some instances data, time, or budget constraints may prevent as complete an analysis of benefits or costs as would be possible in their absence. For example, it may be necessary to use willingness-to-pay estimates for some of the outputs that were obtained for a similar project in another area. Or a market price may be used as a cost estimate even though it is known that there are some monopoly effects present. Any divergence between the operational measures and theoretically appropriate measures of benefits and costs must be clearly indicated in the benefit-cost report. In addition, some notion of whether this will increase or decrease the net present value should be provided.

By way of illustration, let us consider a benefit-cost study of a particular OSH standard, namely, the federal asbestos standard. This standard was developed to control the amount of asbestos dust in the workplace air. Inhalation of this dust can cause a number of serious diseases including several types of cancer. In evaluating the economic effects of the federal asbestos standard, suppose it were feasible to quantify, to some extent, all of the social costs in connection with OSH standards discussed above, namely, (1) compliance costs, (2) enforcement costs, (3) consumers'-surplus losses, and (4) unemployment costs. Suppose further that it was possible to obtain estimates of only the first three benefits, that is, (1) money income gains from reduced morbidity and mortality, (2) savings in treatment resources, and (3) nonmarket productivity gains from reduced morbidity and mortality. This information about which effects were quantifiable and which were not should be clearly stated in the report. In addition, for each effect measured the report should contain a section in which the measurement techniques and the data sources are carefully explained.

As an example of the type of information that can be usefully presented in this section of the benefit-cost report, consider one of the benefits of the asbestos standard, namely, the market productivity gains from reducing the number of asbestos-related deaths. In connection with the construction of a measure for this benefit, the type of information that should be presented includes:

1. The method and data employed in estimating the number of lives saved in various categories (for example, age, sex, income, occupation).

2. The approach to estimating the productivity (income) gains associated with reduced mortality.
3. The method of accounting for anticipated growth in labor productivity over time and for the possibilities that those whose lives are saved might experience some spells of unemployment or might die prematurely from other causes.
4. The discount rate (or rates) used in translating future earnings into present values.
5. The time period employed in the analysis.

Of course, the type of information that is important will vary from study to study, so it is difficult to provide specific guidelines as to what information—and in what detail that information—should be presented. However, as a general rule if an underlying assumption or specific measurement technique is crucial to the analysis, then it clearly should be brought to the attention of the policymaker.

In connection with those assumptions that appear to be more important, the analyst should present the results of sensitivity analyses to show just how crucial these assumptions are to the benefit-cost estimates. If the number of crucial assumptions is "large," judgment will have to be employed in selecting the number of sensitivity analyses to undertake or at least to report in any great detail because the amount of information generated by additional sensitivity analyses increases at a geometric rate. If, for every key assumption or variable (say, the discount rate), the implications of only two alternative values (say, 6 percent and 12 percent) are analyzed, then the number of cells needed to display the resultant data is 2^n where n is the number of key assumptions or variables examined. Thus, the presentation of the results of sensitivity analyses involving ten variables (with two values for each variable) would require over 1000 cells. If each of the ten variables takes on three alternative values, the number of separate pieces of information skyrockets to almost 60,000 (or, to be precise, 3^{10}). Sensitivity analysis can be a very powerful instrument; nevertheless, caution must be exercised to avoid carrying its use too far to provide comprehensible and useful information.

Display of the Benefit-Cost Measures

The next step in the construction of the benefit-cost report is to display the summary benefit-cost measures, either benefit-cost ratios or net present values. The purpose of this display is to convey to the policymaker concise information about both the magnitude and the distribution of the estimated benefits and costs. The display should also contain the results of the sensitivity analyses to assist policymakers in identifying the study's more crucial assumptions.

To illustrate how such information can be displayed, we refer to the results of an actual benefit-cost study of the federal asbestos standard (see Settle 1975). As suggested in the preceding section, this study produced measures of all the social costs associated with OSH standards and some of the social benefits, namely, the market and nonmarket productivity gains and the savings in treatment costs. Estimates of the benefits and costs were made under a variety of assumptions, with the more important ones involving the number of lives saved by the standard, the appropriateness of the nonmarket productivity measure, the discount rate, and the time period.

An illustrative display of the summary benefit-cost measures is presented in table 5-1. This table also reveals the results of sensitivity analyses of the more important assumptions. The asbestos standard was estimated, under certain alternative assumptions, to be capable of saving 630, 1596, or 2563 lives annually. In addition to allowing for these alternative estimates of the number of lives saved, the study also computed the benefit-cost measures for two alternative discount rates—4 and 10 percent—and for two alternative time periods—50 and 100 years. Finally, the benefit-cost measures were calculated with nonmarket productivity gains both included and excluded, the rationale for excluding them being that there is no conventional methodology for measuring such gains thereby rendering their estimates controversial.

An examination of table 5-1 quickly reveals the assumptions to which the results are most sensitive. The benefit-cost ratios are very sensitive to the discount rate: with the 4 percent rate, eleven of twelve ratios exceed unity, while with a 10 percent rate this is true in only four out of twelve cases. The measures are also very sensitive to the treatment of nonmarket productivity gains—their inclusion yields ten of twelve benefit-cost ratios in excess of unity; their exclusion reduces this proportion to five out of twelve. The results of the benefit-cost study are considerably less sensitive to changes in the assumption regarding the number of lives saved, and are quite insensitive to changes in the time period used in the analysis.

How should one interpret a set of benefit-cost statistics (such as those in table 5-1), some of which suggest that a program is efficient and some of which suggest it is inefficient? One approach is for the analyst or the policymaker to essentially ignore the fact that some of the measures offer conflicting implications and select that set of assumptions that appears the most reasonable or appropriate. For instance, if a policymaker feels that public programs of this sort should be evaluated with relatively low discount rates, the fact that relatively high discount rates tend to make the asbestos standard appear inefficient is of little importance. While the analyst is free to select—and probably should explicitly select—the set of assumptions that appear the most appropriate, he should nevertheless present the results of the sensitivity analyses so as to provide policymakers the data necessary to make their own independent judgments and recommendations.

Table 5-1
Alternative Benefit-Cost Ratios for the Federal Asbestos Standard: An Illustration of Sensitivity Analysis

| Discount Rate and Time Period | Lives Saved and Benefit Measures Used | | | | | |
| | 630 Lives Saved | | 1,596 Lives Saved | | 2,563 Lives Saved | |
	Conventional Measures[a]	Unconventional Measures[b]	Conventional Measures	Unconventional Measures	Conventional Measures	Unconventional Measures
4 Percent Rate						
50 years	0.52	3.00	1.20	7.50	1.90	11.90
100 years	1.20	6.90	2.90	17.20	4.50	27.30
10 Percent Rate						
50 years	0.11	0.49	0.26	1.33	0.42	2.11
100 years	0.15	0.68	0.36	1.80	0.58	2.90

[a]The numerator of this measure is the sum of market productivity gains and savings in treatment resources.
[b]The numerator of this measure includes market productivity gains, savings in treatment, and nonmarket productivity gains.

Intangible Effects

The presentation of the measured benefits and costs should not be allowed to obscure the fact that there may remain a number of important but unmeasured or intangible effects. Once the summary statistics are presented, they should be carefully qualified to the extent that some benefits or costs were not measured.

An approach to bringing these omitted effects into the evaluation is to determine the size the unmeasured benefits or costs would have to be to make an "unfavorable" benefit-cost ratio "favorable" or a "favorable" ratio "unfavorable." In connection with the asbestos standard example, the relevant question would be: Could the unmeasured benefits per life saved plausibly be large enough to exceed the measured net cost per life saved (where *net cost* is the difference between the measured social benefits of saving a life and the measured social cost)? Table 5-2 shows the estimates of the net costs per life saved under alternative assumptions regarding the number of lives saved, discount rates, time periods, and treatment of nonmarket productivity gains. Net costs were computed for only those cases involving benefit-cost ratios less than unity. The estimates of net cost per life saved via the asbestos standard range from $22,000 to $158,000 depending upon the underlying assumptions employed. With information of this sort, policymakers should find it easier to come to grips with the problems created by the existence of intangible or unmeasured effects.

Distributional Effects

In addition to presenting information about the economic-efficiency effects of a project, the analyst will often want to provide policymakers with some indication of the income-distributional effects of the project. In fact, policymakers will frequently be more concerned with the distributional effects than with a project's economic efficiency implications.

As we noted in chapter 4, there are a number of classifications that may prove useful in assessing a project's distributional impact. While the categories of interest are likely to differ from one study to another, the classifications commonly used include income, race, sex, age, region, religion, family size, occupation, and educational background. Regardless of the categories selected, a distributional assessment should endeavor to indicate the extent to which the economic well-being of people in those categories has changed as a result of the project. Such an assessment must therefore, in principle, take into account not only the distributional impact of the real benefits and costs, but also the distributional impact of any pecuniary, secondary, or tax effects of the project.

A useful scheme for presenting information about a project's income-distributional effects is illustrated in table 5-3. This particular table is laid out so as to reveal information about a project's distributional consequences in terms

Table 5-2
Estimates of Net Cost Per Life Saved with the Asbestos Standard: Allowance for Intangibles

Discount Rate and Time Period	Lives Saved and Benefit Meaures Used					
	630 Lives Saved		1,596 Lives Saved		2,563 Lives Saved	
	Conventional Measures	Unconventional Measures	Conventional Measures	Unconventional Measures	Conventional Measures	Unconventional Measures
4 Percent Rate						
50 years	$64,000	a				
100 years						
10 Percent Rate						
50 years	$158,000	$78,000	$101,000		$45,000	
100 years	$150,000	$68,000	$54,000		$22,000	

[a]Blank spaces indicate that, under the assumptions indicated, the measured benefits per life saved exceed the measured costs.

Table 5-3
Distribution of Net Discounted Dollar Benefits: An Illustration
(millions of dollars)

Region and Age Group	Income Class						Total
	$0-$4,999		$5,000-$14,000		$15,000 and above		
	White	Nonwhite	White	Nonwhite	White	Nonwhite	
Northeast							
0 to 18 years	−1.0	−1.0	4.0	4.0	3.0	1.0	$10.0
19 to 64 years	−5.0	−6.0	12.0	12.0	13.0	4.0	30.0
65 years and above	−3.0	−2.0	3.0	2.0	4.0	2.0	6.0
North Central							
0 to 18 years							0.0
19 to 64 years							0.0
65 years and above							0.0
South							
0 to 18 years							0.0
19 to 64 years							0.0
65 years and above							0.0
West							
0 to 18 years							0.0
19 to 64 years							0.0
65 years and above							0.0
Total	−9.0	−9.0	19.0	18.0	20.0	7.0	$46.0

of income, age, race, and region. For this particular illustration, we have simply inserted some hypothetical numbers in table 5-3. An examination of these "estimates" of the distributional effects would quickly reveal, for example, that this hypothetical project affects only the northeastern part of the United States and that it benefits middle-to-high income groups at the expense of low-income people. On efficiency grounds, this particular project would appear worthwhile; however, the anticipated distributional effects could well weigh against acceptance of this project. Of course, this type of judgment must be made by policymakers, but without the sort of information presented in table 5-3, an informed policy decision could not be made.

Appendix

Table A–1
The Present Value of $1 for Selected Discount Rates and Time Periods

Year	Discount Rate								
	1%	3%	5%	8%	10%	15%	20%	25%	30%
1	.990	.971	.952	.926	.909	.870	.833	.800	.769
2	.980	.943	.907	.857	.826	.756	.694	.640	.592
3	.971	.915	.864	.794	.751	.658	.579	.512	.455
4	.961	.889	.823	.735	.683	.572	.482	.410	.350
5	.951	.863	.784	.681	.621	.497	.402	.328	.269
10	.905	.744	.614	.463	.386	.247	.162	.107	.073
15	.861	.642	.481	.315	.239	.123	.065	.035	.020
20	.820	.554	.377	.215	.149	.061	.026	.012	.005
25	.780	.478	.295	.146	.092	.030	.010	.004	.001
30	.742	.412	.231	.099	.057	.015	.004	.001	
40	.672	.307	.142	.046	.022	.004	.001		
50	.608	.228	.087	.021	.009	.001			

Table A–2
The Present Value of $1 Per Period for Selected Discount Rates and Time Periods

Year	Discount Rate								
	1%	3%	5%	8%	10%	15%	20%	25%	30%
1	0.990	0.971	0.952	0.926	0.909	0.870	0.833	0.800	0.769
2	1.970	1.913	1.859	1.783	1.736	1.626	1.528	1.440	1.361
3	2.941	2.829	2.723	2.577	2.487	2.283	2.106	1.952	1.816
4	3.902	3.717	3.546	3.312	3.170	2.855	2.589	2.362	2.166
5	4.853	4.580	4.329	3.993	3.791	3.352	2.991	2.689	2.436
10	9.471	8.530	7.722	6.710	6.145	5.019	4.192	3.571	3.092
15	13.865	11.938	10.380	8.559	7.606	5.847	4.675	3.859	3.268
20	18.046	14.877	12.462	9.818	8.514	6.259	4.870	3.954	3.316
25	22.023	17.413	14.094	10.675	9.077	6.464	4.948	3.985	3.329
30	25.808	19.600	15.373	11.258	9.427	6.566	4.979	3.995	3.332
40	32.835	23.116	17.159	11.925	9.779	6.642	4.997	3.999	3.333
50	39.196	25.732	18.256	12.234	9.915	6.661	4.999	4.000	3.333

Bibliography

Anderson, Robert J., Jr., and Crocker, Thomas D. 1971. Air Pollution and Residential Property Values. *Urban Studies,* 8: 171-180.

Arrow, K.J., and Levhari, D. 1969. Uniqueness of the Internal Rate of Return with Variable Life of Investment. *Economic Journal,* 79: 560-566.

Arrow, K.J., and Lind, R.C. 1970. Uncertainty and the Evaluation of Public Investment Decisions. *American Economic Review,* 60: 364-378.

Bailey, M.J. 1959. Formal Criteria for Investment Decisions. *Journal of Political Economy,* 67: 476-488.

Bator, F. 1958. The Anatomy of Market Failure. *Quarterly Journal of Economics,* 72: 351-379.

Baumol, W.J. 1968. On the Social Rate of Discount. *American Economic Review,* 58: 788-802.

Beesley, M. 1965. The Value of Time Spent in Travelling: Some New Evidence. *Economica,* 32: 174-185.

Blaug, M. 1965. The Rate of Return on Investment in Education in Great Britain. *The Manchester School,* 33: 205-261.

Bonnen, J.T. 1968. The Distribution of Benefits from Cotton Price Supports. In *Problems in Public Expenditure Analysis,* ed. S.B. Chase, Jr. Washington, D.C.: Brookings Institution.

Borus, M.E. 1964. A Benefit Cost Analysis of the Economic Effectiveness of Re-training the Unemployed. *Yale Economic Essays,* 4: 371-429.

Broadway, Robin. 1976. Integrating Equity and Efficiency in Applied Welfare Economics. *Quarterly Journal of Economics,* 90: 541-556.

Buchanan, J.M., and Stubblebine, W.C. 1962. Externality. *Economica,* 29: 371-384.

Cesario, F.J. 1976. Value of Time in Recreation Benefit Studies. *Land Economics,* 52: 32-41.

Clawson, M., and Knetsch, J.L. 1971. *Economics of Outdoor Recreation.* Baltimore: Johns Hopkins Press.

Common, M.S. 1973. A Note on the Use of the Clawson Method for the Evaluation of Recreation Site Benefits. *Regional Studies,* 7: 401-406.

Coomber, N.H., and Biswas, A.K. 1972. *Evaluation of Environmental Intangibles.* Bronxville, N.Y.: Genera Press.

Crutchfield, J.A. and Stokes, R. 1973. Benefit Cost Analysis of Export Based Petroleum Activities in Puget Sound. Unpublished paper, Department of Economics, University of Washington.

Coase, R. 1960. The Problems of Social Cost. *Journal of Law and Economics,* 3: 1-44.

Currie, J.M.; Murphy, J.A.; and Schmitz, A. 1971. The Concept of Economic Surplus and its Use in Economic Analysis. *Economic Journal,* 81: 741-799.

Dasgupta, P.; Sen, A.; and Marglin, S. 1972. *Guidelines for Project Evaluation.* New York: United Nations.

Dasgupta, A.K., and Pearce, D.W. 1972. *Cost-Benefit Analysis: Theory and Practice.* London: Macmillan & Co.

Darling, Arthur H. 1973. Measuring Benefits Generated by Urban Water Parks. *Land Economics,* 49: 22–34.

Davidson, P.; Adams, F.G.; and Seneca, J. 1966. The Social Value of Water Recreational Facilities Resulting from an Improvement in Water Quality: The Delaware Estuary. In *Water Research,* ed. A. Kneese and S.C. Smith. Baltimore: Johns Hopkins Press.

Davis, O.A., and Whinston, A.B. 1962. Externality, Welfare and the Theory of Games. *Journal of Political Economy,* 70: 241–262.

Diamond, P. 1968. The Opportunity Cost of Public Investment: Comment. *Quarterly Journal of Economics,* 82: 682–688.

Dorfman, R., ed. 1965. *Measuring the Benefit of Governmental Investments.* Washington, D.C.: Brookings Institution.

Eckstein, O. 1957. Investment Criteria for Economic Development. *Quarterly Journal of Economics,* 71: 56–85.

_____. 1958. *Water Resources Development.* Cambridge, Mass.: Harvard University Press.

Feldstein, M. 1964a. Net Social Benefit Calculation and the Public Investment Decision. *Oxford Economic Papers,* 16: 114–131.

_____. 1964b. The Social Time Preference Discount Rate in Cost Benefit Analysis. *Economic Journal,* 74: 360–379.

Feldstein, M.S., and Flemming, J.S. 1964. The Problem of Time Stream Evaluation: Present Value Versus Internal Rate of Return Rules. *Bulletin of Oxford University Institute of Economics and Statistics,* 26: 79–85.

Fink, F.W.; Buttner, F.H.; and Boyd, W.K. 1971. Final Report on Technical-Economic Evaluation of Air Pollution Corrosion Costs on Metals in the United States to Air Pollution Control Office, Columbus, Ohio: Environmental Protection Agency, Battelle Memorial Institute.

Freeman, A. Myrick, III. 1971. Air Pollution and Property Values: A Methodological Comment. *Review of Economics and Statistics,* 53: 415–416.

_____. 1974. On Estimating Air Pollution Control Benefits from Land Value Studies. *Journal of Environmental Economics and Management,* 1: 74–83.

Fisher, A. 1973. Environmental Externalities and the Arrow-Lind Public Investment Theorem. *American Economic Review,* 63: 722–725.

Fisher, Anthony C.; Krutilla, John V.; and Cicchetti, Charles J. 1972. The Economics of Environmental Preservation: A Theoretical and Empirical Analysis. *American Economic Review,* 62: 605–619.

Goodwin, P.B. 1976. Human Effort and the Value of Travel Time. *Journal of Transport Economics and Policy,* 10: 3–15.

Green, H.A.J. 1961. The Social Optimum in the Presence of Monopoly and Taxation. *Review of Economic Studies,* 29: 66–78.

Hammack, J., and Brown, G.M., Jr. 1974. *Waterfowl and Wetlands: Toward Bioeconomic Analysis.* Baltimore: Johns Hopkins Press.

Harberger, A.C. 1971. Three Basic Postulates for Applied Welfare Economics: An Interpretative Essay. *Journal of Economic Literature,* 9: 785–797.

Harberger, Arnold C., et al., eds. 1972. *Benefit Cost Analysis 1971: An Aldine Annual.* Chicago: Aldine.

Harrison, A.J., and Quarmby, D.A. 1974. The Value of Time. In *Cost Benefit Analysis,* ed. R. Layard. Baltimore: Penguin.

Haveman, Robert H., et al., eds. 1974. *Benefit Cost and Policy Analysis 1973: An Aldine Annual.* Chicago: Aldine.

Haveman, R.H., and Krutilla, J.V. 1958. *Unemployment, Idle Capacity and the Evaluation of Public Expenditure.* Washington, D.C.: Resources for the Future, Inc.

Helliwell, D.R. 1969. Valuation of Wildlife Resources. *Regional Studies,* 3: 41–47.

Henry, C. 1974. Investment Decision Under Uncertainty: The Irreversibility Effect. *American Economic Review,* 64: 1006–1012.

Henderson, P.D. 1965. Notes on Public Investment Criteria in the United Kingdom. In *Public Enterprise,* ed. R. Turvey. Baltimore: Penguin.

Hensher, D.A. 1976. The Value of Commuter Travel Time Savings: Empirical Estimation Using an Alternative Valuation Model. *Journal of Transport Economics and Policy,* 10: 167–176.

Hirshleifer, J. 1958. On the Theory of the Optimal Investment Decision. *Journal of Political Economy,* 66: 329–352.

Howe, C.W. 1971. *Benefit-Cost Analysis for Water System Planning.* Water Resources Monograph, 2. Washington, D.C.: American Geophysical Union.

Howe, J.D. 1976. Valuing Time Savings in Developing Countries. *Journal of Transport Economics and Policy,* 10: 113–125.

James, E. 1969. On the Social Rate of Discount: Comment. *American Economic Review,* 59: 912–916.

Jones-Lee, M.W. 1976. *The Value of Life.* Chicago: University of Chicago Press.

Kneese, Allen V.; Ayres, Robert V.; and d'Arge, Ralph C. 1970. *Economics and the Environment: A Materials Balance Approach.* Washington, D.C.: Resources for the Future, Inc.

Kneese, Allen V., and Bower, Blair T. 1968. *Managing Water Quality: Economics, Technology and Institutions.* Baltimore: Johns Hopkins Press.

———. 1972. *Environmental Quality Analysis: Theory and Method in the Social Sciences.* Baltimore: Johns Hopkins Press.

Kidner, R., and Richards, K. 1974. Compensation to Dependents of Accident Victims. *Economic Journal,* 84: 130–142.

Krutilla, J.V. 1967. Conservation Reconsidered. *American Economic Review,* 57: 777–786.

Krutilla, J., and Cicchetti, C. 1972. Evaluating Benefits of Environmental Resources with Special Application to the Hells Canyon. *Natural Resources Journal,* 12: 1–29.

Krutilla, J.V., and Eckstein, O. 1958. *Multiple Purpose River Development.* Studies in Applied Economic Analysis. Baltimore: Johns Hopkins University Press.

Lave, L.B., and Seskin, E.P. 1970. Air Pollution and Human Health. *Science,* 169: 723–733.

Layard, Richard, ed. 1974. *Cost-Benefit Analysis.* Baltimore: Penguin.

Linzon, Samuel N. 1971. Economic Effects of Sulphur Dioxide on Forest Growth. *Journal of the Air Pollution Control Association,* 21: 81–86.

Leibenstein, H. 1969. Allocative Efficiency versus X-Efficiency. *American Economic Review,* 61: 392–415.

Lesourne, Jacques. 1975. *Cost-Benefit Analysis and Economic Theory.* New York: American Elsevier.

Lind, R.C. 1964. The Social Rate of Discount and the Optimal Rate of Investment: Further Comment. *Quarterly Journal of Economics,* 78: 336–345.

Lipsey, R., and Lancaster, K. 1957. The General Theory of Second Best. *Review of Economic Studies,* 24: 11–32.

Little, I.M.D., and Mirrlees, J.A. 1969. *Manual of Industrial Project Analysis in Developing Countries.* Vol. 2, *Social Cost Benefit Analysis.* Paris: Development Centre of the Organization for Economic Cooperation and Development.

_____. 1972. A Reply to Some Criticisms of the OECD Manual. *Bulletin of the Oxford University Institute of Economics and Statistics,* 34: 153–168.

Maass, A., et al. 1962. *Design of Water Resources Systems.* New York: Macmillan.

Maass, A. 1966. Benefit-Cost Analysis: Its Relevance to Public Investment Decisions. *Quarterly Journal of Economics,* 80: 208–226.

Maler, Karl-Goran. 1971. A Method of Estimating Social Benefits from Pollution Control. *Swedish Journal of Economics,* 73: 121–133.

_____. 1974. *Environmental Economics: A Theoretical Inquiry.* Baltimore: Johns Hopkins University Press.

_____. 1975. Damage Functions and Their Estimation: A Theoretical Survey. In *Environmental Damage Costs.* Paris: Organization for Economic Cooperation and Development.

Maler, K.G., and Wyzga, R.E. 1976. *Economic Measurement of Environmental Damage.* Paris: Organization for Economic Cooperation and Development.

Mansfield, N.W. 1971. The Estimation of Benefits from Recreation Sites and the Provision of a New Recreation Facility. *Regional Studies,* 5: 55–69.

Marglin, S.A. 1963a. The Social Rate of Discount and Optimal Rate of Investment. *Quarterly Journal of Economics,* 77: 95–111.

_____. 1963b. The Opportunity Costs of Public Investment. *Quarterly Journal of Economics,* 77: 274–289.

_____. 1967. *Public Investment Criteria.* Cambridge, Mass.: MIT Press.

Margolis, J. 1955. A Comment on the Pure Theory of Public Expenditure. *Review of Economics and Statistics,* 37: 347–349.

_____. 1969. Shadow Prices for Incorrect or Non-existent Market Values. In *The Analysis and Evaluation of Public Expenditures: The PPB System.* The Joint Economic Committee, Congress of the United States.

McKean, N. 1968. The Use of Shadow Prices. In *Problems in Public Expenditure Analysis,* ed. S.B. Chase, pp. 33–77. Washington, D.C.: Brookings Institution.

Merewitz, L. 1966. Recreation Benefits of Water Resource Development. *Water Resources Research,* 2: 625–640.

Mishan, Ezra J. 1971. Evaluation of Life and Limb: A Theoretical Approach. *Journal of Political Economy,* 79: 687–705.

_____. 1975. *Cost-Benefit Analysis.* 2nd ed. London: George Allen and Unwin.

Mohring, H. 1961. Land Values and the Measurements of Highway Benefits. *Journal of Political Economy,* 69: 236–249.

_____. 1965. Urban Highway Investments. In *Measuring the Benefits of Government Investments,* ed. R. Dorfman. Washington, D.C.; Brookings Institution.

Musgrave, R.A. 1969. Cost-Benefit Analysis and the Theory of Public Finance. *Journal of Economic Literature,* 7: 797–806.

Mushkin, Selma J. 1962. Health as an Investment. *Journal of Political Economy,* 70: 129-157.

Niskanen, William A., et al., eds. 1973. *Benefit Cost and Policy Analysis 1972: An Aldine Annual.* Chicago: Aldine.

Pauly, M.V. 1970. Risk and the Social Rate of Discount. *American Economic Review,* 60: 195-198.

Pearse, Peter H. 1968. A New Approach to the Evaluation of Nonpriced Recreational Resources. *Land Economics,* 44: 87-99.

Pearce, D. The Economics Evaluation of Noise. In *Problems of Environmental Economics.* Paris: Organization for Economic Cooperation and Development.

Peskin, H.M., and Seskin, E.P., eds. 1975. *Cost Benefit Analysis and Water Pollution Policy.* Washington, D.C.: The Urban Institute.

Prest, A.R., and Turvey, R. 1965. Cost-Benefit Analysis: A Survey. *Economic Journal,* 75: 683-735.

Ridker, R.G. 1967. *The Economics of Air Pollution.* New York: Praeger.

Ridker, R.G., and Henning, J.A. 1967. The Determination of Residential Property Values with Special Reference to Air Pollution. *Review of Economics and Statistics,* 49: 246-257.

Roberts, M.J.; Haneman, M.; and Oster, S., 1974. *Study of the Measurement and Distribution of the Costs and Benefits of Water Pollution Control.* Cambridge, Mass.: Harvard University Press.

Schramm, G. 1973. Accounting for Non-economic Goals in Benefit-Cost Analysis. *Journal of Environmental Management,* 1: 129–150.

Sen, A.K. 1961. On Optimizing the Rate of Saving. *Economic Journal,* 71: 479–496.

_____. 1967. Isolation, Assurance and the Social Rate of Discount. *Quarterly Journal of Economics,* 81: 112–124.

_____. 1972. Control Areas and Accounting Prices: An Approach to Economic Evaluation. *Economic Journal,* 82: 486–501.

Settle, Russell. 1975. Benefits and Costs of the Federal Asbestos Standard. Paper presented at a Department of Labor Conference on Evaluating the Effects of Occupational Safety and Health Program, Annapolis, Maryland.

Stevens, J. 1966. Recreational Benefits from Water Pollution Control. *Water Resources Research,* 2: 167–182.

Thaler, R., and Rosen, S. 1976. The Value of Saving a Life: Evidence from the Labor Market. In *Household Production and Consumption,* ed. Nestor E. Terleckyj. Washington, D.C.: National Bureau of Economic Research, vol. 40, pp. 265–298.

Trice, A.H., and Wood, S.E. 1958. Measurement of Recreation Benefits. *Land Economics,* 34: 196–207.

Turvey, R. 1963. On Divergence between Social Cost and Private Cost. *Economica,* 30: 309–313.

U.S. Congress, Subcommittee on Economy in Government of the Joint Economic Committee. 1967. *The Planning-Programming-Budgeting System: Progress and Potentials. Hearings.* 90th Cong., 1st sess., September 14, 19, 20, and 21, 1967 (Washington, D.C.: Government Printing Office).

_____. 1968a. *Economic Analysis of Public Investment Decisions: Interest Rate Policy and Discounting Analysis. Hearings.* 90th Cong., 2nd sess., July 30 and 31 and August 1, 1968 (Washington, D.C.: Government Printing Office).

_____. 1968b. *Interest Rate Guidelines for Federal Decisionmaking. Hearings.* 90th Cong., 2nd sess., January 29, 1968 (Washington, D.C.: Government Printing Office).

Usher, Dan. 1964. The Social Rate of Discount and the Optimal Rate of Investment: Comment. *Quarterly Journal of Economics,* 78: 641–644.

Vickerman, Roger. 1972. The Demand for Non-Work Travel. *Journal of Transport Economics and Policy,* 6: 1–35.

_____. 1974. The Evaluation of Benefits from Recreational Projects. *Urban Studies,* 11: 277–278.

Waddell, Thomas E. 1974. *The Economic Damages of Air Pollution.* Washington, D.C.: Washington Environmental Research Center, Office of Research and Development, United States Environmental Protection Agency.

Weisbrod, B.A. 1960. *Economics of Public Health: Measuring the Impact of Diseases.* Philadelphia: University of Pennsylvania Press.

_____. 1961. The Valuation of Human Capital. *Journal of Political Economy,* 69: 425–436.

_____. 1965. Preventing High School Dropouts. In *Measuring Benefits of Governmental Investments,* ed. R. Dorfman. Washington, D.C.: Brookings Institution.

_____. 1968. Income Redistribution Effects and Benefit-Cost Analysis. In *Problems in Public Expenditure Analysis,* ed. B.S. Chase. Washington, D.C.: Brookings Institution.

Wilkinson, R.K. 1973. House Prices and the Measurement of Externalities. *Economic Journal,* 83: 72–86.

Williams, J.D. 1954. *The Compleat Strategyst.* New York: McGraw Hill.

Zeckhauser, Richard, et al., eds. 1975. *Benefit-Cost and Policy Analysis 1974: An Aldine Annual.* Chicago: Aldine.

Index

About the Authors

Lee G. Anderson received the B.S. in economics from Brigham Young University in 1966 and the Ph.D. from the University of Washington in 1970, also in economics. He is an associate professor of economics and marine studies in the College of Marine Studies at the University of Delaware and he has served on advisory committees for the National Science Foundation and the National Academy of Sciences. Dr. Anderson is the author of *The Economics of Fisheries Management* (Johns Hopkins University Press, 1977) and the editor of *Economic Impacts of Extended Fisheries Jurisdiction* (Ann Arbor Science Publishers, 1977). He has also authored over 20 articles dealing with natural resource economics.

Russell F. Settle received the B.A. in economics from the University of South Florida in 1970 and the M.A. and Ph.D. in economics from the University of Wisconsin-Madison in 1971 and 1974, respectively. He is an associate professor of economics at the University of Delaware. Dr. Settle's specialty is public sector economics, and he has published a number of articles in professional economics journals.

S